# WRITING PHILOSOPHY

*Second Edition*

# WRITING PHILOSOPHY
## A GUIDE FOR CANADIAN STUDENTS

*Lewis Vaughn  &  Jillian Scott McIntosh*

OXFORD
UNIVERSITY PRESS

# OXFORD
UNIVERSITY PRESS

Oxford University Press is a department of the University of Oxford.
It furthers the University's objective of excellence in research, scholarship,
and education by publishing worldwide. Oxford is a registered trade mark of
Oxford University Press in the UK and in certain other countries.

Published in Canada by
Oxford University Press
8 Sampson Mews, Suite 204,
Don Mills, Ontario M3C 0H5 Canada

www.oupcanada.com

**Library and Archives Canada Cataloguing in Publication**

Vaughn, Lewis
Writing philosophy : a guide for Canadian students / Lewis Vaughn &
Jillian Scott McIntosh.—2nd Canadian ed.

Includes index.

ISBN 978–0–19–544674–6

1. Philosophy.—Authorship. I. McIntosh, Jillian Scott II. Title.

B52.7.V38 2012      808.06'61      C2012-904009-6

Cover image: J-P Lahall/Peter Hall/Getty Images

This book is printed on permanent (acid-free) paper ∞.

Printed and bound in the United States of America

1 2 3 4 — 16 15 14 13

# ❧ Contents ❧

# ❧ Preface ❧

This text aspires to help philosophy teachers address a big problem: the conflict between trying to teach course content and dealing with students who are ill-prepared to write papers on that content. The dilemma is acute because writing is both a valuable teaching tool and a vehicle for assessing understanding. Using class time to explain the unique demands of philosophical writing, however, can divert time and attention from the real meat of a course. (Grading a batch of poorly written papers, of course, is no fun either.) No book by itself can teach good writing, just as no book can be a substitute for the teacher. *Writing Philosophy*, nevertheless, tries to come as close as possible to the ideal of a brief, self-guided manual that covers the basics of philosophical essay writing and encourages rapid learning with minimal teacher input.

This kind of assault on the "writing problem" requires that the text be maximally self-sufficient, that it lack very few components that instructors might have to supply. It therefore covers fundamental skills in reading philosophy, composing text, outlining papers, evaluating arguments, citing sources, avoiding plagiarism, detecting fallacies, and formatting finished papers. Teachers, of course, may want to add material to these essentials—but they may not need to.

A guiding principle of this text is that simplicity serves inexperienced writers best; it is better to focus on the basics than to present a dizzying array of options or to discuss sophisticated nuances. Even with uncomplicated writing assignments in philosophy, beginners will have plenty to think about. If they can produce one fairly simple but clear paper, they will be more likely to excel when confronted with greater writing challenges.

## Main Features

- An *introductory chapter on reading philosophy.* This text begins where many teachers think that instruction on writing philosophy *should* begin—with reading philosophy. This coverage consists of a general introduction to philosophy, rules for increasing understanding of philosophical texts, and instruction on writing paraphrases and summaries. This chapter is part of the book's quick-start approach: it gets students writing immediately so that, by Chapter 5, they can attempt full-blown papers.
- A *discussion of exegetical and expository writing.* This chapter helps students see the point of such writing, whether in a stand-alone essay or as part of an argumentative essay, and includes rules covering how to write such content effectively and persuasively.
- *Step-by-step instructions on how to write argumentative essays.* Instructions cover the entire essay-writing process, from formulating a thesis to creating an outline to writing a final draft. These are supplemented with model essays, outlines, introductions, and conclusions.
- A *rulebook format that encapsulates core principles of good writing.* Like the classic *Elements of Style,* this text tries to distill the most helpful writing advice into simple rules that the student can easily remember and readily apply—and that the teacher can refer to in providing feedback on student papers. Rules cover essay organization, sentence structure, documentation styles, plagiarism, grammar, and usage. There are, for example, eleven rules on style and content, eight rules on effective sentences, four rules (and multiple instructions) on quotations and documentation, and nine rules on proper word choice.
- A *chapter on recognizing, reading, and evaluating arguments.* Rules also cover the analysis of premises and conclusions, deductive and inductive arguments, and common argument patterns.
- A *chapter on recognizing and avoiding logical fallacies.* The emphasis is on fallacies that are likely to show up in student writing—straw man, ad hominem, appeal to ignorance, hasty generalization, genetic fallacy, appeal to popularity, false dilemma, begging the question, and others.
- *Full coverage of plagiarism and proper acknowledgement of sources.* There are instructions here on how to use three standard

documentation systems. The information includes recent developments in citing Internet material and is meant to be detailed enough to allow students to document their papers properly without having to consult other books or websites on citing sources.

- A *reference guide to common writing errors and skills.* Chapters 8 and 9, together with Appendix C, constitute a reference section covering basic writing mistakes in sentence construction, writing style, and word choice. Inexperienced writers can read this reference guide straight through or refer to it when specific writing questions arise (by either checking the table of contents or using the book's detailed index). More advanced students can use the guide to hone their writing skills or to refresh their memories about writing fundamentals.
- *Guidelines for formatting papers.* Appendix A provides instructions and examples to help beginners format their papers using specifications generally used in the humanities.

## Teaching Strategies

Instructors will differ in how they use *Writing Philosophy* depending on how much class time they want to devote to writing instruction. Here are some of the possibilities:

- Assign the reading of Chapters 1–5 right away; devote a small block of class time to lectures or discussions on Chapters 1 and 2 (possible assignments: writing paraphrases and summaries). Devote another small block of class time to writing an argumentative essay (the subject of Chapter 5). Assign the remaining chapters (6–9).
- Assign the reading of Chapters 1–7 during the first weeks of the course along with the writing of paraphrases, summaries, outlines, essay introductions, and, finally, complete papers. Devote some class time to answering questions about the material. Recommend the use of the reference guide (Chapters 8–9 and the appendices).
- At the beginning of the course, assign the reading of the entire book. Throughout the course, assign the writing of several essays of increasing difficulty, providing feedback on each with references to relevant parts of the text.

# ❧ Preface to the ❧
# Second Canadian Edition

This edition differs from the first in that it includes a short chapter on exegetical writing, motivated by the fact that some instructors assign purely exegetical papers, plus the vast majority of argumentative essays require some exegesis to set things up. What is exegetical writing? Why engage in it? How does one do it effectively? What is its relationship to argumentative writing?

Also in this edition, more attention has been paid to the use of the Internet, including mention of possible perils. Students are not usually in a position to discern good websites from bad, and this is made explicit. In addition, there is more detailed advice on how to cite. In particular, new conventions for citing the Internet (such as using a DOI) are introduced. Also, APA-style citation is included. This style is becoming the style of choice for many philosophers, and was left out of the previous edition of this book.

The section on "how to format your paper" has been expanded to include discussion of the use and placement of an abstract.

The concepts in Chapter 2 on arguments have been re-worked slightly to allow an important distinction to be more easily made: the distinction between an argument with all true premises and an argument with premises all of which are reasonable for a given person to accept. Many students find this a subtle distinction, so it helps to have the terminology introduced in this book facilitate discussion of this distinction if the instructor so chooses.

I would like to thank Lewis Vaughn (again) for writing the original edition—I have, since I initially encountered it, made it required reading in all my lower-division essay courses and recommended reading in my upper-division ones. It is an excellent book, and I was delighted to have the opportunity to tailor it to the Canadian market. I would also like to thank the anonymous reviewers and the editorial staff at Oxford University Press for their helpful suggestions for both the first and the second editions. And I am grateful for the opportunity to improve the book with this second edition.

Finally, I would like to repeat my thanks to my now-retired colleague and mentor, Peter Horban. Peter personifies clarity of expression, excellence in pedagogy, and generosity of spirit. I hope this second edition comes close to living up to his standards.

Jillian Scott McIntosh
February 2012

# ❦ PART 1 ❦

# READING AND WRITING

# ❦ 1 ❦
# How to Read Philosophy

To write philosophy, you must be able to read philosophy. To read philosophy—to really read it with understanding and appreciation—you must cast off the misconceptions that make philosophy seem barren or impenetrable or trifling. You must abandon the myths about philosophy that cast it as a dark and distant island, way out of the normal shipping lanes and hardly worth an hour's sailing.

You must also be willing to give philosophy a chance, to look for what countless people have seen in philosophy throughout the ages. Philosophical ideas have changed the world, altered lives, inspired cultures, and driven history. You must try to understand what the fuss is about.

Philosophers—those who know philosophy best—would tell you that the study of philosophy is well worth the trouble. But you should not take their word for it. You should try to explore the conceptual terrain for yourself. This chapter helps you get started.

## Asking the Big Question

So, what exactly is philosophy?

Whatever else philosophy may be, it is a discipline, a field of inquiry. It examines the most fundamental of beliefs—those that structure our lives, shape our worldview, and underpin all academic pursuits. A physiologist may want to know how our brains work, but a philosopher asks a deeper question—for example, whether the brain is the same thing as the mind. A lawyer may study how the court has ruled in cases of euthanasia, but a philosopher asks whether euthanasia is ever morally permissible. A medical scientist may want to know how a human fetus develops, but a philosopher asks what the moral status of the fetus is. An astrophysicist may study the big bang (the cataclysmic explosion thought to have brought the universe into being), but a philosopher asks whether the big bang shows that God caused the universe to exist. Someone may wonder if lying to protect a friend is right or wrong, but a philosopher asks what makes any action right or wrong. You may find yourself reflecting on the horrific evils of war and famine; a philosopher asks if these evils can be squared with the existence of an all-powerful, all-knowing, and all-good God.

These points contradict a common myth about philosophy—the notion that it is a trivial endeavour, a pretentious exercise in small matters that have no bearing on issues in real life. Obviously, if philosophy tackles questions such as those just listed, it deals with very important issues indeed. Philosophy often raises difficult questions, but "difficult" is not the same as "trifling," and seriously trying to answer the questions does not make you pretentious.

Notice that philosophy is not primarily concerned with what causes you to have the particular beliefs you do. Strong emotions, peer pressure, and cultural influences may cause you to adopt certain opinions, but the important philosophical question is whether those opinions are *worthy of belief*. A belief is worth believing, or accepting, if there are good reasons to accept it. The better the reasons for acceptance, the more likely the belief is to be true. Philosophy is a critical and wide-ranging search for understanding, and as such it is perfectly suited to this kind of deeper assessment of beliefs.

Sometimes people use the word *philosophy* in a narrower (or at least different) sense, as in "My philosophy is that we should live and let live." Here, *philosophy* means something like **worldview**. A worldview is a set of fundamental ideas that help us make sense of a wide range of important issues in life. A worldview is the framework that shapes a person's thinking; it underpins what a person thinks both is the case and should be the case.

An interesting fact about worldviews is that we all have one. We all have certain ideas about what exists and what doesn't, what kinds of actions are right or wrong, and what type of claims we can know or not know. Even the rejection of all worldviews is a worldview. A vital question, then, is not whether we have a worldview but whether our worldview is worth having—whether the beliefs that constitute our worldview are true. Since our lives are guided by this worldview, it had better be good! Using philosophy in the broad sense is the best way we have of evaluating a "philosophy" in this narrower sense.

We are born into this world at a particular place and time, steeped in the ideas and values of a particular culture, handed ready-made beliefs that may or may not be true and that we may never think to question. Philosophy helps us rise above this predicament, past the narrowness and obstructions of our prejudices, to reach a better vantage point. It helps us examine our unexamined beliefs in the light of reason and try to see what's real and true. By using the methods of philosophy, we may learn that some of our beliefs stand on solid ground and others do not. In either case, through philosophy our beliefs become truly and authentically our own, and we are more fully in control of the course we take in life.

As you can see, philosophy as a discipline is both broad and deep—but it is not static. More than anything else, philosophy is a process—a careful, systematic investigation of fundamental beliefs. When we get involved in the process, we are "doing philosophy." We do what great philosophers and ordinary people have done for thousands of years: We make systematic use of critical reasoning to explore answers to basic questions, to clarify the meaning of concepts, and to formulate or evaluate logical arguments.

Clarifying the meaning of concepts is important because we cannot evaluate the worth of a belief or statement until we understand what it means. Often we may think that we understand a concept—until we look at it more closely. Philosophy gives us the tools to take this closer look. The larger and more characteristic part of doing philosophy, however, is the assessment of arguments. As you will see in Chapter 2, the term **argument** in philosophy does not refer to heated disagreements or emotional squabbles. In philosophy, an argument is a statement, or **claim**, coupled with other statements that are meant to support it. The statement to be supported is the **conclusion**, and the statements meant to do the supporting are the **premises**. The premises are meant to provide reasons for believing that the conclusion is true. A good argument gives us good reasons for accepting a conclusion; a bad argument fails to provide good reasons. In philosophy—and in any other kind of rational inquiry—accepting a statement without good reasons is an elementary mistake in reasoning. Believing a statement without good reasons is a recipe for error; believing a statement for good reasons increases your chances of uncovering the truth. Arguments are therefore a driving force behind the advancement of knowledge in all fields.

When we do philosophy, then, we grapple with arguments—we try to either (1) devise an argument to support a statement, or (2) evaluate

## ❧ The Divisions of Philosophy ❧

Philosophy divides its subject matter into four categories. Each category is a branch of inquiry in its own right with many subcategories and many points of overlap with other categories. Here's a brief rundown of the kinds of questions asked in each division:

**Metaphysics** is the study of reality, an inquiry into the fundamental nature of the universe and the things in it. Although it must take into account the findings of science, metaphysics generally focuses on fundamental questions that science alone cannot answer. Questions of interest: Is mind the same thing as body? Do people have free will? Is there a God? What is the nature of causality? Does science (attempt to) tell us about a mind-independent world?

**Axiology** is the study of value, including both aesthetic value and moral value. Questions of interest: What makes an action right (or wrong)? What moral principles should guide our actions and choices? What things are intrinsically good? What makes a work of art a good one? Are moral or aesthetic standards objective or subjective? How should goods be distributed in a just society?

**Epistemology** is the study of knowledge. Questions of interest: What is knowledge? Does knowledge require certainty? When are we justified in saying that we know something? Is experience a source of knowledge? Is reason? Do we know anything at all?

**Logic** is the study of inference patterns. Questions of interest: What are the rules for drawing correct inferences? What is the nature and structure of deductive arguments? What is the nature and structure of inductive arguments? How do we justify our inferential practices?

an argument to see whether it provides good grounds for accepting its conclusion. Some of this process, of course, gets done in serious discussions with others or in a philosopher's solitary thoughts. But a great deal of philosophy occurs on paper, where writers try to create or assess arguments in essays or articles or other kinds of texts. The purpose of this book is to help you learn how to handle this task—and eventually to excel at it.

The attempt to write good philosophy papers has consequences. First, it leads to discoveries—some unsettling and some splendid. Through the process of devising and evaluating arguments, you may come to see that a cherished belief is unsupportable, or that the arguments of others are faulty, or that arguments that you once found dubious are actually solid. You may achieve remarkable insights into an issue that always puzzled you. Probably for most people, *writing* philosophy is the best way to *think* about philosophy. Second, you become a better thinker. Philosophical thinking is systematic, analytic, productive thinking and is useful in many everyday situations and fields of study. Third, you come to better understand and appreciate the great thinkers of the past. Grasping the significance of their powerful ideas can be deeply satisfying, even liberating. Great ideas have a way of lifting people up from their customary perspective on the world, enabling them to see farther than they thought possible.

## A Different Kind of Reader

In some ways, reading philosophy is like reading the literature of many other fields. It requires a good deal of abstract thought, often involves difficult concepts or extraordinary propositions, and can be intimidating to those who approach the subject for the first time. But in other ways, reading philosophy is distinctive. You are not simply trying to glean facts from it as you might if you were reading a science text or a technical report. Nor are you following a storyline as if you were reading a mystery novel (although philosophy papers sometimes contain their share of mysteries). In most cases, you are tracing the steps in an argument, trying to see what conclusion the writer wants to prove and whether he or she succeeds in proving it. Along the way, you may encounter several premises with their accompanying analyses, clarifications, explanations, and examples. You may even run into a whole chain of arguments. In the end, if you have read well and the writer has written well, you are left not with a new set of data or a story ending, but with a realization—maybe a revelation—that a conclusion is, or is not, worthy of belief.

The best way to learn how to read philosophy well is to read it *often*. You will probably get plenty of chances to do that in your current philosophy course. A few rules, however, may help shorten the learning curve. As you read, keep the following in mind.

### Rule 1-1    Approach the Text with an Open Mind

If you are studying philosophy for the first time, you may well find a good bit of the material difficult, strange, or exasperating—sometimes all three at once. That's normal. Philosophy explores the rugged frontiers of our knowledge of fundamental things, so it's likely to seem daunting or unfamiliar. There's also an excellent chance that your first visits to this terrain will occasionally be infuriating because you disagree with what you read.

There is no shame in experiencing any of these reactions. They come with the territory. But if you are to make any headway in philosophy and write good papers, you need to counteract these attitudes and feelings. Remember, philosophy at its best is a fair-minded, fearless search for truth. Anything that interferes with this noble quest must be overcome and cast aside. Here is some advice on how to do that:

- Avoid making a judgment about an essay's ideas or arguments until you fully understand them and have fairly considered them. Make sure you are not reading with the intent to prove the conclusions false (or true). Be open to the possibility that the essay could give you good reasons to change your mind about something.
- Try to maintain a neutral attitude toward the writer, presuming that he or she is neither right nor wrong, neither sinner nor saint. Don't assume that everything a renowned philosopher says must be true, and don't presuppose that everything a philosopher you dislike says must be false. Give the writer the same attention and respect that you would give a friend who is discussing a serious issue with you.
- If you are reading the work of a famous philosopher and you find yourself thinking that his or her ideas are obviously ridiculous, think again. The odds are good that you are misunderstanding what you read. It is wiser to assume that the text offers something of value (even if you disagree with it) and that you need to read more carefully.
- Once you do make a judgment about the value of a writer's ideas, ask yourself what reasons you have to support that judgment. If you cannot think of any reasons, your judgment is suspect. Reconsider your evaluation.

### Rule 1-2    Read Actively and Critically

Philosophical reading is intense. It cannot be rushed. It cannot be crammed. It cannot be done while your mind is on automatic pilot. You must follow the twists and turns of an argument (or several arguments) from premises to conclusion, often through digressions and speculations, ultimately arriving at an understanding of the writer's work. You want to end up knowing what the writer is trying to prove and whether he or she has successfully proved it. The route requires concentration and perseverance.

Philosophical reading is *active* reading. You must take your time and ask yourself what key terms and passages mean, how the argument is structured, what the central thesis is, where the premises are, how certain key ideas are related, whether the main conclusion conflicts with propositions you know are true, even how the material compares with other philosophical writing on the same subject.

Philosophical reading is also *critical* reading. You ask not just what something means, but whether a statement is true and the reasoning solid. You ask whether the conclusion really follows from the premises, whether the premises are true, whether the analysis of a term really makes sense, whether an argument has been overlooked, whether an analogy is weak, whether there are counterexamples to key claims, and whether the claims agree with other things you have good reason to believe.

When we read fiction, we must often "suspend disbelief" for the sake of the story. We discard any doubts we might have about the realism of the narrative and pretend that the story could actually happen. But when you read philosophy, you must never suspend your disbelief in this way. The whole point of the exercise is to discover whether various claims are worthy of acceptance.

Reading philosophy actively and critically takes time—a lot of time. You read slowly and deliberately, and probably do a lot of note-taking and highlighting. Speed-reading is out of the question. Skimming is pointless. Even if you read at a snail's pace, you will probably need to reread the material, and then reread again, as many times as necessary to fully understand the text.

### Rule 1-3    Identify the Conclusion First, Then the Premises

When you first begin reading philosophical texts, they may seem to you like dark thickets of propositions into which you may not enter without losing your way. But it's really not that bad. In argumentative writing, you can depend on there being, well, an argument: a conclusion backed by premises. There could, of course, be several arguments that support the main argument, and the arguments could be complex, but these sets of conclusion-plus-premises serve as signposts. To penetrate the thicket, then, you must first identify the argument (or arguments). And the key to doing that is to find the conclusion first, then look for the premises. (Chapter 2 details how to identify arguments of all kinds, even when they are surrounded by a great deal of non-argumentative prose.)

By finding the main conclusion, you thereby identify the central point of the essay, which gives the most important clue to the function of all the other text. Once you uncover the point that the writer wants to prove, finding the supporting premises becomes much easier. And when you isolate the premises, locating the text that explains and amplifies the premises gets easier too. Therefore, the first—and most important—question you can ask about a philosophical essay is, "What claim is the writer trying to prove?"

### Rule 1-4    Outline, Paraphrase, or Summarize the Argument

Understanding an essay's argument is so important that testing whether you really "get it" is crucial. You can test your grasp of the argument by outlining, paraphrasing, or summarizing it. If you can lay out an argument's premises and conclusion in an outline, or if you can accurately paraphrase or summarize the argument, you probably have a pretty good understanding of it. Very often students who think they comprehend an argument are surprised to see that they cannot devise an adequate outline or summary. Such failures suggest that, although outlining, paraphrasing, or summarizing may seem unnecessary to some, they are not—at least not to those new to philosophy.

Outlining an argument means identifying the premises and the conclusion and arranging them in an outline pattern that reveals their relationships. Each of these components should be stated in a complete sentence. In such a pattern, each premise is listed in order on a single line followed by the last line, which is the conclusion. Like this:

- Premise 1
- Premise 2
- Premise 3
- Conclusion

If the premises are in turn supported by other arguments (in which they occupy the role of conclusion), the outline may look like this:

- Main premise 1
  Supporting premise a
  Supporting premise b

- Main premise 2
  Supporting premise a
  Supporting premise b
  Supporting premise c
- Main premise 3
- Conclusion

Other models are possible; especially common are cases in which there is a subconclusion (supported by premises) used as a premise in a grander argument.

You may state each of your outline points in the same language used in the essay or in your own words. Remember, this kind of outline is not a sketch of the entire essay, just of the argument itself. (An outline of the whole essay may include other points besides the parts of the argument.) Very often, however, the outline of the argument will be virtually identical to an outline of the entire essay. In any case, other parts of the essay (for example, introductory background information or extended concluding remarks) will make sense to you only if you fully understand the argument.

To some students, writing a paraphrase or summary of the argument is more helpful than creating an outline. In a **paraphrase**, you create your own accurate facsimile of the argument, rephrasing it in your own words. In a **summary**, you paraphrase and condense, distilling the argument into fewer words than the original. By successfully paraphrasing or summarizing, you demonstrate that you do indeed understand the argument. (See the next section, "Writing a Paraphrase or Summary" and Chapter 4 for more guidance.)

### Rule 1-5    Evaluate the Argument and Formulate a Tentative Judgment

When you read philosophy, understanding what you've read is just the first step. You also must do something that many beginners find both difficult and alien: make an informed judgment about what you read. Simply reiterating what the writer has said will not do. Your judgment is what matters here. Mainly, this judgment is your evaluation of the argument presented by the writer: (1) does the conclusion follow from the premises? and (2) are the premises reasonable for you to believe (i.e., do you think them true)? Only when the answer is yes to both questions can you say that the conclusion of the argument is worthy of your acceptance. This kind of evaluation is precisely what your

## Five Common Mistakes in Reading Philosophy

1. Reading philosophy the same way you would read a technical report or a novel.
2. Prejudging the text's argument or author.
3. Failing to evaluate what you read.
4. Trying to speed-read or skim.
5. Not reading actively and critically.

instructor expects when he or she asks you to critique an argumentative essay in philosophy.

A philosophical text, of course, contains more than just a bare-bones argument. Often a considerable amount of space is devoted to explaining the background or history of the topic being addressed, elaborating on each of the premises, discussing the implications of the argument's conclusion, and answering possible criticisms of the essay's main points. Certainly you must take these into account when you are reading and evaluating a philosophical text (see Chapter 4 on Exegetical and Expository Essays). But often your primary task is to arrive at an honest and well-reasoned assessment of the text's central claim.

# Writing a Paraphrase or Summary

There are three reasons why you should try to master paraphrasing or summarizing an essay's argument. The first one you already know: it increases your understanding. Second, you need these skills to do well on essay exams. Third, in just about every philosophy paper you write, you will have to restate or condense arguments. Paraphrasing and summarizing are required.

In good essays, writers often paraphrase or summarize a source because their own wording is clearer than that of the original author. They sometimes summarize a passage because the author's original is too long to quote verbatim yet all its main points are worth mentioning. Whether they add a paraphrase or summary, however, they are careful to cue the reader about it. Just as quotations should be introduced properly and explained in a paper, so must paraphrases and summaries. Readers should never have to guess whose ideas are being put forth, what a paraphrase or summary means, or how it relates to the rest of the paper.

The first step here is understanding the text. Do not begin writing until you have read the entire piece and think that you understand it well. In other words, do not try to paraphrase or summarize until you have followed *Rule 1-2* (read actively and critically).

Paraphrasing is a matter of rewriting text—accurately representing the text's meaning but doing so in your words, not in a barely disguised rendition of the author's words. A paraphrase is not a condensation, so in most cases any paraphrase you produce should contain close to the same number of words as the author's original.

In paraphrasing, you try to capture the gist of passages—perhaps just the paragraph that contains the argument in a nutshell, or the section of the paper that discusses a major point, or even the entire essay, point by point. If you want in-depth understanding of what a philosopher is saying, there is no better way than to paraphrase the entire essay.

Consider this passage, the beginning of one of the most discussed (and shortest!) papers in philosophy:

**Passage**[1]

[1]  Various attempts have been made in recent years to state necessary and sufficient conditions for someone's knowing a given proposition. The attempts have often been such that they can be stated in a form similar to the following:[1]

(a) S knows that P   IFF   (i) P is true,
                             (ii) S believes that P, and
                             (iii) S is justified in believing that P.

For example, Chisholm has held that the following gives the necessary and sufficient conditions for knowledge:[2]

(b) S knows that P   IFF   (i) S accepts P,
                             (ii) S has adequate evidence for P, and
                             (iii) P is true.

Ayer has stated the necessary and sufficient conditions for knowledge as follows:[3]

(c) S knows that P  IFF  (i) P is true,
                          (ii) S is sure that P is true, and
                          (iii) S has the right to be sure that P is true.

I shall argue that (a) is false in that the conditions stated therein do not constitute *sufficient* conditions for the truth of the proposition that S knows that P. The same argument will show that (b) and (c) fail if "has adequate evidence for" or "has the right to be sure that" is substituted for "is justified in believe that" throughout.

[2] I shall begin by noting two points. First, in that sense of "justified" in which S's being justified in believing P is a necessary condition for S's knowing that P, it is possible for a person to be justified in believing a proposition that is, in fact, false. Secondly, for any proposition P, if S is justified in believing P, and P entails Q, and S deduces Q from P and accepts Q as a result of this deduction, then S is justified in believing Q. Keeping these two points in mind, I shall now present two cases in which the conditions stated in (a) are true for some proposition, though it is at the same time false that the person in question knows that proposition.

1  Plato seems to be considering some such definition at *Theatetus* 201, and perhaps accepting one at *Meno* 98.

2  Roderick M. Chisholm, *Perceiving: A Philosophical Study*, Cornell University Press (Ithaca, New York, 1957), p. 16.

3  A.J. Ayer, *The Problem of Knowledge*, Macmillan (London, 1956), p. 34.

To understand this passage, you must realize that "IFF" is short-hand for "if and only if." Keeping this in mind, as well as the fact that the passage does not include the argument, consider this paraphrase.

## Paraphrase 1

Gettier writes that many attempts have been made to define the conditions under which it is true that a person knows a proposition. One popular view is that S knows that P if and only if P is true, S believes that P, and S is justified in believing that P. Gettier is going to argue that this definition, as with others like it, is false because the conditions stated are not sufficient for S to know that P. Before presenting his argument, he notes that he is understanding "justified" in such a way that a person can be justified in believing a proposition that is false, and that if somebody validly deduces a proposition from another proposition that person is justified in believing, then the person will be justified in believing the deduced proposition.

This paraphrase is not acceptable. It is fairly accurate but mimics the words and phrases of the original too closely. It repeats, for example, some parts word for word: "S knows that P if and only if P is true, S believes that P, and S is justified in believing that P," "justified in believing a proposition that is false." Also, some sentences that are not verbatim are obviously and blatantly modelled after Gettier's. The close mimicry of this passage is a problem for two reasons. First, it diminishes the opportunities for better understanding of the text because it is mere repetition instead of thoughtful, thorough recasting. Second, the paraphrase constitutes plagiarism. It repeats many of Gettier's words verbatim without enclosing them in quotation marks, and it closely apes his ideas and sentence patterns. (See *Rules 7-2* and *7-3*.)

Here is a better paraphrase:

**Paraphrase 2**

Gettier [citation] argues against a family of analyses of the concept of knowledge, all of which place three conditions on knowledge. For example, "S knows that P IFF [if and only if] (i) P is true, (ii) S believes that P, and (iii) S is justified in believing that P" [exact citation]. The conditions are intended to be individually necessary and jointly sufficient for it to be true that S knows that P. Gettier argues that all the conditions can be met, yet the case not be one of knowledge; hence, meeting all three conditions is not sufficient for knowing. Before presenting his examples, he explicitly makes two assumptions: a proposition does not need to be true in order for a person to be justified in believing it, and valid inference preserves justification. [exact citation] This latter assumption is that if one validly infers a proposition from another proposition that one is justified in believing, one will be justified in believing the deduced proposition.

This paraphrase is accurate and does not improperly borrow Gettier's words or sentence patterns. It gives clear indication that the ideas have been derived from Gettier and puts material that is difficult to paraphrase in quotation marks. (The material in square brackets was inserted to clarify—square brackets in a quotation indicate that those words were not in the original.) In an actual paper, accurate citation, including pages numbers, would be provided. (See Appendix B for citation styles.) This paraphrase indicates engagement with, and understanding of, the material under consideration.

Let's look at the rest of the essay:[2]

### Case I

[3]   Suppose that Smith and Jones have applied for a certain job. And suppose that Smith has strong evidence for the following conjunctive proposition:

> (d) Jones is the man who will get the job, and Jones has ten coins in his pocket.

Smith's evidence for (d) might be that the president of the company assured him that Jones would in the end be selected, and that he, Smith, had counted the coins in Jones's pocket ten minutes ago. Proposition (d) entails:

> (e) The man who will get the job has ten coins in his pocket.

Let us suppose that Smith sees the entailment from (d) to (e), and accepts (e) on the grounds of (d), for which he has strong evidence. In this case, Smith is clearly justified in believing that (e) is true.

[4]   But imagine, further, that unknown to Smith, he himself, not Jones, will get the job. And, also, unknown to Smith, he himself has ten coins in his pocket. Proposition (e) is then true, though proposition (d), from which Smith inferred (e), is false. In our example, then, all of the following are true: (*i*) (e) is true, (*ii*) Smith believes that (e) is true, and (*iii*) Smith is justified in believing that (e) is true. But it is equally clear that Smith does not *know* that (e) is true; for (e) is true in virtue of the number of coins in Smith's pocket, while Smith does not know how many coins are in Smith's pocket, and bases his belief in (e) on a count of the coins in Jones's pocket, whom he falsely believes to be the man who will get the job.

### Case II

[5]   Let us suppose that Smith has strong evidence for the following proposition:

> (f) Jones owns a Ford.

Smith's evidence might be that Jones has at all times in the past within Smith's memory owned a car, and always a Ford, and that Jones has just offered Smith a ride while driving a Ford. Let us imagine, now, that Smith has another friend, Brown, of whose whereabouts he is totally ignorant. Smith selects three place-names quite at random, and constructs the following three propositions:

(g) Either Jones owns a Ford, or Brown is in Boston.
(h) Either Jones owns a Ford, or Brown is in Barcelona.
(i) Either Jones owns a Ford, or Brown is in Brest-Litovsk.

Each of these propositions is entailed by (f). Imagine that Smith realizes the entailment of each of these propositions he has constructed by (f), and proceeds to accept (g), (h), and (i) on the basis of (f). Smith has correctly inferred (g), (h), and (i) from a proposition for which he has strong evidence. Smith is therefore completely justified in believing each of these three propositions. Smith, of course, has no idea where Brown is.

[6]    But imagine now that two further conditions hold. First, Jones does *not* own a Ford, but is at present driving a rented car. And secondly, by the sheerest coincidence, and entirely unknown to Smith, the place mentioned in proposition (h) happens really to be the place where Brown is. If these two conditions hold then Smith does *not* know that (h) is true, even though (*i*) (h) is true, (*ii*) Smith does believe that (h) is true, and (*iii*) Smith is justified in believing that (h) is true.

[7]    These two examples show that definition (a) does not state a *sufficient* condition for someone's knowing a given proposition. The same cases, with appropriate changes, will suffice to show that neither definition (b) nor definition (c) do so either.

The remainder of the essay consists of two examples that are supposed to serve to show that the analyses of knowledge are flawed. Let's look at a paraphrase:

## Paraphrase 3

Gettier provides two situations that he takes to be counter-examples to the received view of knowledge as justified true belief. In the first, Smith and Jones are both in the running for a job, and Smith justifiably believes that Jones will get the job and that Jones has ten coins in his pocket. He validly infers from this that the man who will get the job has ten coins in his pocket. This is a justified true belief, but there is a twist. It is Smith who will get the job, and he just happens to have ten coins in his pocket. In the second situation, Smith jus-tifiably believes that Jones owns a Ford. The rule of addition, which Smith knows, states that from any proposition, a disjunction with that proposition as one of its disjuncts follows validly. That is, it is not possible for a proposition to be true yet a disjunction with it as one of its disjuncts to be false, no matter what the truth value of the other disjunct. Smith doesn't know where his friend Brown is, but be-lieves all the disjunctions he can think of involving Brown's where-abouts provided the other disjunct is that Jones owns a Ford. He justifiably believes that Jones owns a Ford or Brown is in Barcelona. But again, there is a twist. This disjunction is true, but not for the reason that Smith accepts it. Jones does not own a Ford, but Brown is in Barcelona. Gettier concludes that in both cases Smith does not *know* the true propositions he justifiably believes.

This is an accurate paraphrase that does not inappropriately borrow or mimic Gettier's words or phrasing. (See Chapter 2 for some discus-sion of valid inferences.)

A summary must accurately capture a text's main ideas in just a few words. You should be able to summarize the main points of an entire essay (that is, the premises and conclusion) in fewer than 150 words. Those words, of course, must be your own. This particular essay is very short, so a summary of it can also be very short:

> Gettier argues that knowledge cannot be understood to be justified true belief on the grounds that there are examples of justified true beliefs that are not instances of knowledge.

## Applying the Rules

Let's apply the reading rules we set out earlier in the chapter.

*Rule 1-1.* This little essay is well suited to testing students' ability to approach a piece of philosophical writing with an open mind. Most students do not come to philosophy with views about how to understand the concept of knowledge, let alone worries about the adequacy of proposed analyses, so it is not the case that most stu-dents need to combat any tendencies to have prejudged the issues. However, precisely because they likely do not have preconceived ideas, students need to be open to both the analyses offered and Gettier's criticisms of them. You must engage with the text in a spirit of intellectual curiosity.

*Rules 1-2 and 1-3.* Reading and re-reading the essay actively and critically would help you see that: (1) the thesis statement (the conclusion of the author's argument) concerns the viability of standard understandings of the concept of knowledge—Gettier thinks they are flawed in a particular way; (2) some paragraphs are not part of the essay's argument but simply introduce the topic, explain the view to be critiqued, or state the assumptions the author is making; (3) the essay argues by way of (alleged) counterexamples, and (4) the author gives evidence that the family of views under consideration is one that has adherents, so the author's criticism is important.

*Rule 1-4.* An outline of the essay's argument would look like this:

Premise • There are cases of justified true belief that are not instances of knowledge.

Conclusion • Analyses of knowledge that construe it as justified true belief do not provide sufficient conditions.

*Rule 1-5.* The essay puts forth a deceptively simple argument. We say "deceptively" because philosophers are *still* responding to this article! With this essay, as with any other, your main priority in evaluating the argument is to determine whether the conclusion follows from the premise and whether the premise is reasonable for you to accept. Gettier's conclusion does indeed follow: if there are examples of justified true beliefs that are not knowledge, then being a justified true belief cannot be sufficient for being knowledge. (See Chapter 2 for more on how to assess argument structure.)

Should you accept the premise? That is, are the examples Gettier gives actually instances of justified true belief? If they are not, then they are not counter-examples to the analyses he is considering. Note that it won't do to argue against Gettier by claiming you have a different conception of knowledge. His attack is very focused: the only legitimate responses are, in broad strokes, to argue that his counter-examples are not genuine instances of justified true belief (perhaps by attacking his assumptions), to deny that the cases are not instances of knowledge, or to accept his conclusion and hence to look for an analysis of knowledge that is immune to what has come to be called "Gettierization."

# ❦ QUICK REVIEW ❦
## Reading Philosophy

- Philosophy is not primarily concerned with what causes you to have particular beliefs; it focuses on whether those beliefs are worth having.

- Philosophy helps you evaluate your worldview.

- Through philosophy, your beliefs can become truly and authentically your own, and you can be more fully in control of your life.

- In philosophy, an argument is a statement, or claim, coupled with other statements that are meant to support that statement.

- The productive reading of philosophy requires an open mind, an active and critical approach, and the identification of the conclusion and premises.

- Outlining, paraphrasing, or summarizing can enhance your understanding of a philosophical essay.

*For discussion:*

- What is the difference between paraphrasing and summarizing?
- When and why would you quote instead of paraphrase or summarize?
- Why should sources of ideas be cited?
- In what sense do the authors intend the word "prejudices" in this chapter (p. 4)?
- What sorts of writing do you read slowly? Quickly? Absent-mindedly? Intently?

*For further information:*

- Several other handbooks on reading and writing philosophy exist, but they, like this one, are effective only if you dive into some philosophy and try your hand at reading and writing it. But they can still be useful, so poke around in used bookstores or your friends' bookshelves. Be aware that some key terms may be defined differently.

- See your college's or university's website for information on avoiding plagiarism.

- See also your library's website for that, for the distinction between paraphrase, summary, and quotation, and for information on proper citation.

- Read Chapter 7 of this book ("Using, Quoting, and Citing Sources").
- See www.sfu.ca/~horban/qps1.htm for information on quoting, paraphrasing, and summarizing.[3]
- Most importantly, consult with your instructor, whose expectations and directions overrule suggestions and sources mentioned here.

## Notes

1. Edmund L. Gettier, "Is Justified True Belief Knowledge?" *Analysis* 23 (1963), pp. 121–3. Reproduced with permission of Oxford University Press.
2. Excerpted from Gettier (op. cit.) 121–3. Reproduced with permission of Oxford University Press.
3. Peter Horban, "Quoting, Paraphrasing, and Summarizing" © 2005.

# ❧ 2 ❧
# How to Read and Evaluate an Argument

To a large extent, to read and write philosophy is to read and write arguments, for logical argument is at the heart of philosophy. When we do philosophy, we are usually either evaluating or constructing arguments. The philosophy that we read will most likely contain arguments, and our understanding of the text will hang on our ability to identify and understand them. Most often the quality of the philosophical essays we write will depend on the quality of the arguments we craft. Learning the fundamentals of logical argument, then, is a prerequisite for making sense out of philosophy and writing good philosophy papers. That is why this is one of the longest chapters in the book. It will get you going in the right direction by showing you how to pick out arguments from passages of non-argumentative prose, assess different kinds of arguments, devise good ones yourself, and recognize defective arguments when you see them.

## Premises and Conclusions

A statement, or claim, is an assertion that something is or is not the case—a declarative sentence, grammatically speaking. It is the kind of utterance that, to use a philosophical term of art, expresses a proposition. Propositions are either true or false (and not both). These are statements—they express propositions:

- A tree is growing in the quad.
- I am shocked and dismayed.

- $2 + 2 = 4$
- Time heals all wounds.
- The universe is 15 billion years old.

These two statements express the same proposition:

- Vancouver est une ville en Colombie-Britannique.
- Vancouver is a city in British Columbia.

These, however, are not statements—they do not express propositions:

- Why is a tree growing in the quad?
- Why are you shocked and dismayed?
- Stop being stupid.
- Holy cow!

The first two sentences are questions; the third, a command or request; and the fourth, an exclamation. These are not the kind of things that express propositions—they are not, to put it loosely, true or false.[1]

An argument is a combination of statements in which *some* are intended to combine in support of *one*. That is, one set of statements is meant to provide reasons for believing that another statement is true. The statements supposedly giving support are known as **premises**; the statement supposedly being supported is known as the **conclusion**.

All rational beings try to determine how strongly to believe particular statements. A principle in philosophy is that the strength of our belief in a statement should depend on the strength of the reasons for believing it. A statement supported by strong reasons merits strong acceptance. A statement supported by weaker reasons deserves weaker acceptance. The analysis of arguments is the primary method we use to discover how much credence to give statements and reasons. This essential method matters not only in philosophy but in all fields of knowledge.

By now you will have realized that logical arguments are not arguments in the ordinary sense of shouting matches, heated debates, or angry squabbles. In philosophy and other kinds of intellectual exploration, an argument is a set of statements containing a conclusion and premises meant to support it. Arguments in the ordinary sense are beside the point.

We must also distinguish between logical argument and persuasion. They are not synonymous. Presenting a good argument is a way to demonstrate that a statement is warranted, that the conclusion is worthy of acceptance. The argument's persuasiveness or lack thereof is a completely separate matter. On the one hand, a good argument may not persuade a person to accept the conclusion. On the other hand, you may be able to persuade someone to accept a statement through the use of psychological or rhetorical trickery—for example, emotional language, fallacious appeals, threats, or deceit. But if you do, you will not have shown that the statement is worthy of belief because you will not have provided any reasons for accepting it.

Here are some arguments:

### Argument 1

Chivalry is dead. My instructor says so.

### Argument 2

If Calgary scores, a white horse will gallop down the sidelines. They will definitely score. So, a white horse galloping down the sidelines is a sure thing.

### Argument 3

Ninety-two per cent of the students are under the age of 60. Joan is a student, so she's under the age of 60.

### Argument 4

All men are mortal. Socrates is a man. Therefore, Socrates is mortal.

Now let's spell out the premises and conclusion in each one:

### Argument 1

[Conclusion] Chivalry is dead. [Premise] My instructor says so.

### Argument 2

[Premise] If Calgary scores, a white horse will gallop down the sidelines. [Premise] Calgary will score. [Conclusion] A white horse will gallop down the sidelines.

### Argument 3

[Premise] Ninety-two per cent of the students are under the age of 60. [Premise] Joan is a student. [Conclusion] Joan is under the age of 60.

### Argument 4

[Premise] All men are mortal. [Premise] Socrates is a man. [Conclusion] Socrates is mortal.

Notice that these arguments differ in the placement and number of their parts. In *Argument 1*, the conclusion comes first, then the premise. In the other three arguments, the conclusion comes last. *Argument 1* has one premise, but *Arguments 2, 3,* and *4* have two premises each. The point is that arguments come in all kinds of configurations. An argument could have one premise, or two, or ten, or more. Sometimes a premise or even the conclusion goes unstated, leaving the reader to fill in the blank (more on uncovering implicit statements later). Regardless of their structure, all arguments must have a conclusion and at least one premise. As long as this requirement is met, arguments can vary all over the map.

Now take a look at this passage:

The stock market has tanked. Brokers are skittish. The TSX is the lowest it's been in 10 years. We're pretty scared about all this.

Is there an argument here? If you think so, where is the conclusion? Where are the premises? Alas, this little observation about the stock market is not an argument. The passage consists of a series of statements with no conclusion in sight. There is no statement that other statements are supporting.

It is easy enough, however, to turn these statements into an argument. Look:

### Argument 5

The world of stocks and bonds is in for a rough ride because the stock market has tanked, brokers are skittish, and the TSX is the lowest it's been in 10 years.

This passage is now a bona fide argument. The conclusion is, "The world of stocks and bonds is in for a rough ride." The three statements that follow support the conclusion.

Being able to distinguish arguments from non-argumentative material is a valuable skill, and the sooner you master it the better. You will often encounter passages that seem to conceal an argument somewhere but do not actually have one at all. Many people (are you one of them?) think that if they clearly and firmly state their beliefs,

---

### Four Common Mistakes in Evaluating Arguments

1. Failing to distinguish between the logical structure of an argument and the acceptability of its premises.
2. Thinking that merely stating views is the same thing as presenting an argument.
3. Thinking that persuading someone to accept a claim is the same thing as presenting an argument.
4. Failing to distinguish between arguments and non-argumentative material.

---

they have given an argument. Sometimes they fill whole essays with well-made statements and interesting points in an attempt to make a strong case—but no argument is presented. Despite all the verbiage, such essays fail to provide the reader with a single good reason to accept any assertion. As we have seen, a collection of unsupported statements does not an argument make. For there to be an argument, at least one statement must provide reasons for accepting another. Now consider this passage:

> Kravitz is absolutely the worst premier this province has ever had. I don't understand how anyone can read about the premier's exploits in the paper and still support him. Haven't the citizens of this province had enough scandal and corruption in the premier's office? I am aghast at Kravitz's outrageous behaviour and obvious ineptness.

Has the writer presented an argument? Once again, no. This passage is certainly an expression of displeasure, even anger and disgust. But we find no claim supported by reasons. With some major alterations, however, we can turn the passage into an argument:

#### Argument 6

> Kravitz is absolutely the worst premier this province has ever had. He has embezzled money from the province's coffers. He has ruined the province's economy. And he has used his office to persecute those he doesn't like. I am aghast at Kravitz's outrageous behaviour and obvious ineptness.

If we laid out the argument so we can more clearly see its structure (that is, if we outline it), it would look like this:

Premise 1 • Kravitz has embezzled money from the province's coffers.
Premise 2 • Kravitz has ruined the province's economy.
Premise 3 • Kravitz has used his office to persecute those he doesn't like.
Conclusion • Kravitz is absolutely the worst premier this province has
ever had.

Notice that the last sentence of the passage is not shown in this argument outline. That's because it does not form part of the argument.
It does not support the conclusion; it simply expresses the writer's
reaction to the premier's misdeeds.

Logical arguments often come packaged with all sorts of non-
argumentative material—introductory remarks, explanations,
redundancies, descriptions, asides, examples, and more. The trick
is to separate the premises and conclusion from all the other stuff.
Once you pinpoint those, spotting the extraneous material is fairly
straightforward.

As noted in *Rule 1-3*, the simplest way to locate an argument is to
find its conclusion first, then its premises. Zeroing in on conclusions
and premises can be a lot easier if you keep an eye out for indicator words—words that indicate that a conclusion or premise may be
nearby. Arguments 2 through 5 contain several indicator words; go
back and see if you can pick them out.

The following indicator words may alert you to a conclusion:

| | |
|---|---|
| consequently | as a result |
| thus | hence |
| therefore | so |
| it follows that | which means that |

The following indicator words may alert you to a premise:

| | |
|---|---|
| in view of the fact | assuming that |
| because | since |
| due to the fact that | for |
| the reason being | given that |

Remember that indicator words do not guarantee the presence of conclusions and premises. They can be helpful clues, though.

One final wrinkle: we mentioned earlier that some arguments
have unstated, or implicit, premises. A few even have unstated conclusions. For example:

*Argument 7*

> Any judge who supports the unrestricted use of security certificates is an enemy of the Charter of Rights and Freedoms. Judge Simpson is definitely an enemy of the Charter of Rights and Freedoms.

The conclusion of this argument is "Judge Simpson is definitely an enemy of the Charter of Rights and Freedoms," and the only premise is the first statement. There seems to be a leap of logic from premise to conclusion. Something is missing. The conclusion follows logically only if we insert an additional premise to bridge the gap, something like this:

*Argument 7 (expanded)*

> Any judge who supports the unrestricted use of security certificates is an enemy of the Charter of Rights and Freedoms. Judge Simpson supports the unrestricted use of security certificates. Therefore, Judge Simpson is definitely an enemy of the Charter of Rights and Freedoms.

Now we can see both the stated premise as well as the one left unmentioned, and we can conduct a complete evaluation.

When you're evaluating an argument, you should always bring any implicit claims out into the open. It makes evaluation possible and also helps you to avoid falling into a logical trap. Often premises that are left unstated are dubious or false. You should never let questionable premises slide by unnoticed.

## Judging Arguments

In Chapter 1, we saw the importance of approaching a philosophical text with an open mind (*Rule 1-1*); reading actively and critically (*Rule 1-2*); identifying the conclusion first, then the premises (*Rule 1-3*); outlining, paraphrasing, or summarizing the argument (*Rule 1-4*); and evaluating the argument and formulating a tentative judgment (*Rule 1-5*). Chances are you are most intimidated by *Rule 1-5*. You need not be. The following rules elaborate on *Rule 1-5* and detail more techniques for systematically sizing up arguments, even complex ones that are buried in a tangle of extraneous material.

### Rule 2-1   Know the Basics of Deductive and Inductive Arguments

As we saw in Chapter 1, a good argument gives us good reasons for accepting a conclusion; a bad argument fails to provide good reasons.

To tell the difference—and to do so consistently—you need to under-stand the different forms that arguments can take.

Arguments are either **well-formed** or **ill-formed**. A well-formed argument has premises that, if true, would support the conclusion. Well-formed arguments come in two basic types: deductive and inductive. **Deductive** arguments aim to offer logically conclusive support for their conclusions. If a deductive argument actually manages this task, it is **valid**. If it fails, it is **invalid**. If a deductive argument is valid, it possesses this peculiar characteristic: if its premises are true, its conclusion is true. No exceptions. In a valid argument, it is impossible for the premises to be true and the conclusion false. Notice that *valid* is not a synonym for *true*. A valid argument is simply one that has a structure or form guaranteeing a true conclusion if the premises are true. A valid argument, then, is one whose conclusion strictly follows from the premises.

Take a look at this simple deductive argument:

**Argument 8**

> All soldiers are brave.
> Jocelyn is a soldier.
> Therefore, Jocelyn is brave.

In this argument, you can see that if the premises are true, then the conclusion cannot be false. The form of the argument—not its specific content—is what guarantees this outcome. Notice that the first premise is actually false (and you have no way to tell about the second premise, since you don't know to whom "Jocelyn" refers), but the argument is still valid. We could plug completely different state-ments into this argument, but as long as the form stays the same, the argument would remain valid.

Consider this deductive argument:

**Argument 9**

> If stealing harms people, then it [stealing] is morally wrong.
> Stealing harms people.
> Therefore, stealing is morally wrong.

This argument is also valid. If it is true that *if stealing harms people then it is morally wrong*, and if it is also true that *stealing harms people*, then the conclusion *stealing is morally wrong* must be true as well. If this strikes you as painfully obvious, don't be concerned—your logic instincts are in fine working order!

Traditionally, philosophers have symbolized the form of deductive arguments by using letters to stand for parts of the argument. The form of *Argument 9*, then, can be symbolized this way:

If $p$, then $q$.
$p$.
Therefore, $q$.

Here, the letters $p$ and $q$ represent the two "atomic" (simple) statements in the argument. The first premise is a compound statement, made up of the two atomic statements $p$ and $q$, and a connective (in this case, "if...then"). We could insert any statements we want into this valid form, and it would still be the case that if the premises were true, the conclusion would be true.

Unlike deductive arguments, **inductive** arguments aim to support their conclusions, but with less than 100 per cent certainty. If an inductive argument succeeds in providing such support, it is said to be **cogent**. In a cogent argument, if the premises are true, it is probable (but not certain) that the conclusion is true. If an inductive argument fails to provide such support for its conclusion, it is said to be *ill-formed*.

As with a valid argument, a cogent argument is one whose conclusion follows from its premises; however, it is possible for the premises to be true and the conclusion false. (Inductive arguments are invalid, but they are not ill-formed—think about the definitions.)

Consider these two inductive arguments:

### Argument 10

Almost all of the students at this school vote Liberal.
Therefore, Maria, who is a student here, votes Liberal.

### Argument 11

Ninety per cent of the Conservatives I know own an SUV.
Therefore, 90 per cent of all Conservatives are SUV owners.

*Argument 10* is cogent. If it is true that almost all the students at the school vote Liberal, then it is likely that Maria votes Liberal too. Yet it is possible for the premise of *Argument 10* to be true and the conclusion false.

*Argument 11*, on the other hand, is ill-formed. Even if 90 per cent of Conservatives known by some arbitrary person own a sport-utility vehicle, it does not follow that 90 per cent of all Conservatives are SUV owners. The relatively small sample of Conservatives known by this person does not allow us to generalize to millions of them.[2]

We can now be more precise about the characteristics of good arguments. Good arguments must be well-formed—that is, they must be either *valid* or *cogent*. But arguments that we find rationally persuasive must also have premises that we think are reasonable to accept. Such arguments are **strong** for us. An argument is not strong for us (does not give us good reasons for accepting its conclusion) unless it is valid or cogent and we have reason to think its premises are true.

A valid deductive argument that in fact has true premises (whether we recognize this or not) is said to be **sound**. There is no agreed-upon term for a cogent inductive argument with true premises. At any rate, what interests us is well-formed arguments whose premises are reasonable for us to accept—ones whose premises we have reason to believe are true.[3]

## Rule 2-2    Determine Whether the Conclusion Follows from the Premises

Usually, the first step in assessing the worth of an argument is to determine whether the conclusion follows from the premises—that is, whether the argument is valid or cogent. If the conclusion does not follow from the premises, then the argument cannot give you good reason to accept the conclusion. As we saw above, such an argument can be called *ill-formed*. In this case, the argument should not be strong for you—even if you think the premises are true (and even if the premises are in fact true!).

Very often, when you examine an argument, you will see right away whether the conclusion follows from the premises. At other times, you may have to think about the argument's structure for a while, and, in the case of induction, other things you know. But in many cases, you will need some help in sizing up the argument—the kind of help offered in the following pages.

Fortunately, deductive arguments often occur in certain classic patterns. The forms or structures of the arguments show up again and again. We introduce three common structures here.

Consider again *Argument 9*:

### Argument 9

> If stealing harms people, then it [stealing] is morally wrong.
> Stealing harms people.

Therefore, stealing is morally wrong.

We symbolized the argument this way:

If $p$, then $q$.
$p$.
Therefore, $q$.

This kind of argument is known as **affirming the antecedent** (or, in Latin, *modus ponens*), since one of its premises "affirms" the antecedent of the conditional that is the other premise. A conditional is an "if…then" statement; when in its standard form, the first part (after the "if" but before the "then") is the antecedent. What follows the "then" is the consequent. Any argument using this pattern is valid, no matter what the statements say. (The order of the premises is irrelevant.)

Another classic pattern is **denying the consequent** (or, in Latin, *modus tollens*). Consider the following arguments:

### Argument 12

If the cat is on the mat, then she [the cat] is asleep.
She [the cat] is not asleep.
Therefore, she [the cat] is not on the mat.

### Argument 13

If the mind is identical to the brain, then damaging the brain will damage the mind.
But damaging the brain will not damage the mind.
Therefore, the mind is not identical to the brain.

Denying the consequent, then, is symbolized this way:

If $p$, then $q$.
Not $q$.
Therefore, not $p$.

Any argument having this form is valid. Again, the order of the premises does not matter.

Here's a slightly more involved form known as **hypothetical syllogism**:

### Argument 14

If the cat is on the mat, then she [the cat] is asleep.

If she [the cat] is asleep, then she [the cat] is dreaming.
Therefore, if the cat is on the mat, then she [the cat] is dreaming.

The hypothetical syllogism is symbolized this way:

If *p*, then *q*.
If *q*, then *r*.
Therefore, if *p*, then *r*.

Any argument having this form is valid. Once again, the order of the premises does not matter, but be careful not to get fooled. Sometimes it is helpful to re-arrange them to make sure the pattern is what you think it is.

---

### ❧ QUICK REVIEW ❧
## Valid Conditional Argument Forms

| | |
|---|---|
| Affirming the Antecedent (modus ponens) | If *p*, then *q*.<br>*p*.<br>Therefore, *q*. |
| Denying the Consequent (modus tollens) | If *p*, then *q*.<br>Not *q*.<br>Therefore, not *p*. |
| Hypothetical Syllogism | If *p*, then *q*.<br>If *q*, then *r*.<br>Therefore, if *p*, then *r*. |

---

There are also common invalid forms. If you know these, it's easier to spot bad arguments. Here's one called *denying the antecedent*:

**Argument 15**

If the Parliament Buildings are in Montreal, they are in Canada.
The Parliament Buildings are not in Montreal.
Therefore, the Parliament Buildings are not in Canada.

Denying the antecedent is symbolized this way:

If *p*, then *q*.
Not *p*.
Therefore, not *q*.

It is invalid because an argument with this form can have a false conclusion despite having true premises.

Another common invalid form is the following, called *affirming the consequent*:

**Argument 16**

> If the Parliament Buildings are in Montreal, they are in Canada.
> The Parliament Buildings are in Canada.
> Therefore, the Parliament Buildings are in Montreal.

Affirming the consequent is symbolized this way:

> If *p*, then *q*.
> *q*.
> Therefore, *p*.

Again, it is invalid because an argument with this form may have true premises and a false conclusion.

Many other invalid forms exist, but *Arguments 15* and *16* are among the most deceptive in that they are the most likely to be thought valid when they are not.

The best way to use these argument forms to evaluate deductive arguments is to memorize them so you can more easily identify examples when you encounter them. If the form of the deductive argument you are evaluating matches one of the classic valid forms, it is also valid; if it matches an invalid form, it is likewise invalid.

---

### ❧ QUICK REVIEW ❧
### Invalid Conditional Argument Forms

| | |
|---|---|
| Denying the Antecedent | If *p*, then *q*.<br>Not *p*.<br>Therefore, not *q*. |
| Affirming the Consequent | If *p*, then *q*.<br>*q*.<br>Therefore, *p*. |

---

Inductive arguments also have distinctive forms, and being familiar with some of them can help you evaluate the arguments. Let's look at three common forms of inductive arguments.

In **enumerative induction,** we arrive at a generalization about an entire group of things after observing just some members of the group. Here are some typical enumerative inductive arguments:

*Argument 17*

> Every pizza I've bought from this restaurant has been delicious.
> Therefore, all pizzas at this restaurant are delicious.

*Argument 18*

> All the hawks that I have observed in this wildlife sanctuary have had red tails.
> Therefore, all the hawks in this sanctuary have red tails.

*Argument 19*

> Sixty per cent of the Haligonians I have interviewed in various parts of Halifax are pro-choice.
> Therefore, 60 per cent of all Haligonians are pro-choice.

As you can see, enumerative induction has this form:

> *x* per cent of the observed members of group *a* have property *p*.
> Therefore, *x* per cent of all members of group *a* have property *p*.

The observed members of the group constitute a sample of the entire group. Based on what we know about this sample, we generalize to all the members. How do we know whether such an argument is cogent? Everything depends on the sample. If the sample is large enough and representative enough, we can safely assume that a generalization drawn from it would be an accurate reflection of the whole group of members, and hence, barring other factors, the argument will be strong for us.[4] A sample is likely to be representative of an entire group if each member of the group has an equal chance of being included. Generally, the larger the sample, the greater the probability that it accurately reflects the nature of the whole group. In complicated situations such as national opinion polls, experts will dispute what counts as a reliable sample size. Often in cases of enumerative induction, though, common sense tells us when a sample is much too small.

We do not know how many pizzas from the restaurant are in the sample mentioned in *Argument 17.* If the number is several dozen and the pizzas were bought over a period of weeks or months, the sample is probably sufficiently large and representative. If so, the argument is cogent. That is, if we have reason to believe the sample is well chosen, the argument is, barring outside information, strong for us. Likewise, in *Argument 18* we don't know the size of the sample or how it was obtained. But if the sample was drawn from all the likely spots in the sanctuary where hawks live, and if several hawks were observed in each location, the sample is probably adequate—and the argument is cogent. If we believe it cogent and have no conflicting information, the argument is strong for us. In *Argument 19*, if the sample consists of a group of Haligonians that the interviewer happens to know, the sample is definitely inadequate and the argument should be weak for us. But if the sample consists of several hundred people, chosen in such a way as to represent all Haligonians, then the sample would be good enough to allow us to generalize about the whole population with largely successful results.

In the argument form known as **analogical induction** (or argument by analogy), we reason in this fashion: Two or more things are similar in several ways; therefore, they are probably similar in another way. Consider this argument:

### Argument 20

Humans can walk upright, use simple tools, learn new skills, and devise deductive arguments.
Chimpanzees can walk upright, use simple tools, and learn new skills.
Therefore, chimpanzees can devise deductive arguments.

This argument says that because chimpanzees are similar to humans in several respects, they probably are similar to humans in one further respect.

Here's an argument by analogy that has become a classic in philosophy:

### Argument 21

A watch is a complex mechanism with many parts that seem arranged to achieve a specific purpose—a purpose chosen by the watch's designer. In similar fashion, the universe is a complex mechanism with many parts that seem arranged to achieve a specific purpose. Therefore, the universe also has a designer.

We can represent the form of an argument by analogy in this way:

$x$ has properties $p1$, $p2$, and $p3$, plus the property $p4$.
$y$ has properties $p1$, $p2$, and $p3$.
Therefore, $y$ has property $p4$.

The cogency of an analogical induction depends, in part, on the relevant similarities between the two things compared. The more relevant similarities there are, the greater support they offer to the conclusion, hence the more cogent the argument is. *Argument 20* notes several similarities. But there are some unmentioned dissimilarities. Most of us know that the brain of a chimpanzee is smaller and less complex than that of a human, and that this difference probably inhibits higher intellectual functions in chimpanzees, such as logical argument. *Argument 20* likely is, then, weak for most of us. A common response to *Argument 21* is to consider it weak too because, although the universe resembles a watch in some ways, in many other ways it does not.

The third type of inductive argument is known as **inference to the best explanation,** a kind of reasoning that we all use daily and that is at the heart of scientific investigations. Recall that an argument gives us reasons for believing that something is the case. An explanation, on the other hand, states how or why something is the case. It attempts to clarify or elucidate, not offer proof. For example:

1. Su-Feh definitely understood the material, since she could answer every question on the test.
2. Su-Feh understood the material because she has a good memory.

The first sentence is an (incomplete) argument. The conclusion is "Su-Feh understood the material," and the premise given is "she could answer every question on the test." The second sentence, however, is an explanation; it does not present reasons for believing something. Instead, it presents a reason for why something is the way it is (why Su-Feh understood the material). In the appropriate context, it is assumed that Su-Feh understood the material, and discussion involves why this is the case. Such discussions play a crucial role in inference to the best explanation.

In this type of inductive argument, we begin with premises about a phenomenon or state of affairs to be explained. Then we reason from those premises to an explanation for that state of affairs. We try to produce not just any old explanation but the best explanation among several possibilities. The best explanation is the one most likely to be true. Indeed, the argument concludes that the preferred explanation *is* true. For example:

**Argument 22**

Megan flunked her philosophy course. The best explanation for her failure is that she didn't read the material. Therefore, she didn't read the material.

**Argument 23**

Ladies and gentlemen of the jury, the defendant was found with the murder weapon in her hand, blood on her clothes, and the victim's wallet in her pocket. We have an eyewitness putting the defendant at the scene of the crime. The best explanation for all these facts is that the defendant committed the murder. There can be very little doubt—she's guilty.

Here's the form of inference to the best explanation:

Phenomenon $q$.
$e$ provides the best explanation for $q$.
Therefore, $e$ is true.

This pattern is not valid, since being the best explanation is not the same as being the true explanation. But the argument is cogent. If the premises are true, they support the conclusion. If we have reason to think they are true, then the argument is strong for us, provided we have no information that would rationally overturn our confidence.

The biggest challenge in using inference to the best explanation is determining which explanation is the best. Sometimes it's easy. If our car has a flat tire, we may quickly uncover the best explanation for such a state of affairs. If we see a nail sticking out of the flat, and there is no obvious evidence of tampering or of any other extraordinary cause (that is, we find no good alternative explanations), we would feel safe concluding that the best explanation is that a nail punctured the tire.

In more complicated situations, we may need to act as scientists do to evaluate explanations or theories — use special criteria to sort through the possibilities. Scientists call these standards the "criteria of adequacy." Despite this fancy name, these criteria are basically just common-sense standards that you have probably used yourself.

One of these criteria is called *conservatism*. This criterion says that, all things being equal, the best explanation or theory is the one that fits best with what is already known or established. For example, if a friend of yours says—in all seriousness—that she can fly to the moon without using any kind of rocket or spaceship, you probably aren't going to believe her (and might even think that she needs psychiatric help). Your reasons for doubting her would probably rest on the criterion of conservatism—that what she says conflicts with everything science knows about space flight, human anatomy, aerodynamics, laws of nature, and much more. It is logically possible that she really can fly to the moon, but her claim's lack of conservatism—the fact that it conflicts with so much of what we already know about the world—casts serious doubt on it.

### Rule 2-3    Determine Whether the Premises Are True

When you are carefully reading an argument (whether in an essay or some other context), you will be just as interested in whether the premises are true as in whether the conclusion follows from the premises. If the writer is conscientious, he or she will try to ensure that each premise is either well supported or in no need of support (because the premise is obvious or agreed to by all parties). The needed support will come from the citing of examples, statistics, research, expert opinion, and other kinds of evidence or reasons. This arrangement means that each premise of the primary argument may be a conclusion supported in turn by premises citing evidence or reasons. In any case, you as the reader will need to evaluate carefully the truth of all premises and the support behind them.

When you are trying to write a good argument, one that will be rationally compelling for its readers, the story will be much the same. You will want to provide good reasons to your readers for accepting the premises when you believe that simply explaining your premises is not enough. You must provide support for each premise that requires it and ensure that the support is adequate and reliable. (See Chapter 7 and Appendix B for guidance on using and citing sources.)

## Applying the Rules

Let's read and evaluate an argument in an extended passage, applying the rules discussed in this chapter and the previous one. The following excerpt focuses on one aspect of a famous argument for the existence of God. Read it and review the comments that follow.

*The Design Argument*
Nigel Warburton

[1]   One of the most frequently used arguments for God's existence is the Design Argument, sometimes also known as the Teleological Argument (from the Greek word "telos" which means "purpose"). This states that if we look around us at the natural world we can't help noticing how everything in it is suited to the function it performs: everything bears evidence of having been designed. This is supposed to demonstrate the existence of [a] Creator. If, for example, we examine the human eye, we see how its minute parts all fit together, each part cleverly suited to what it was apparently made for: seeing. . . .

[2]   Even if, despite the objections mentioned so far, you still find the Design Argument convincing, you should notice that it doesn't prove the existence of a unique, all-powerful, all-knowing, and all-good God. Close examination of the argument shows it to be limited in a number of ways.

[3]   First, the argument completely fails to support monotheism—the view that there is just one God. Even if you accept that the world and everything in it clearly shows evidence of having been designed, there is no reason to believe that it was all designed by one God. Why couldn't it have been designed by a team of lesser gods working together? After all, most large-scale, complex human constructions such as skyscrapers, pyramids, space rockets, and so on, were made by teams of individuals, so surely if we carry the analogy to its logical conclusion it will lead us to believe that the world was designed by a group of gods.

[4]   Second, the argument doesn't necessarily support the view that the Designer (or designers) was all-powerful. It could plausibly be argued that the universe has a number of "design faults": for instance, the human eye has a tendency to short-sightedness and to cataracts in old age—hardly the work of an all-powerful Creator wanting to create the best world possible. Such observations might lead some people to think that the Designer of the universe, far from being all-powerful, was a comparatively weak God or gods, or possibly a young god experimenting with his or her powers. Maybe the Designer died soon after creating the universe, allowing it to run down of its own accord. The Design Argument provides at least as much evidence for these conclusions as it does for the existence of the God described by the Theists. So the Design Argument alone cannot prove that the Theists' God rather than some other type of God or gods exists.[5]

To be successful in evaluating the argument, we must approach the text with an open mind (*Rule 1-1*) and read actively and critically

(*Rule 1-2*), striving for full understanding. After that, our top priority is to identify the conclusion and the premises (*Rule 1-3*) and then outline, paraphrase, or summarize the whole argument (*Rule 1-4*). Our ultimate task is to evaluate the argument and formulate a tentative judgment about it (*Rule 1-5*). And that means having a good understanding of different types of arguments (*Rule 2-1*) so we can determine whether the argument is valid or strong (*Rule 2-2*) and whether the premises are true (*Rule 2-3*).

After reading the excerpt a few times, we can see that the author's purpose is to present one argument against another—the so-called "Design Argument." In paragraph 1, he states that the design argument says that because everything in the world looks as though it has been designed, it must have a designer, namely God. But in paragraph 2, Warburton asserts that the design argument doesn't prove what many people think it does. It doesn't prove that the designer is God in the monotheistic sense—an all-powerful, all-knowing, all-good supreme being. He backs up this assertion in paragraphs 3 and 4, giving two reasons for believing that the creator doesn't necessarily have to be anything like the Judeo-Christian or Islamic God.

After reading the excerpt, we should go back and look for indicator words. When we do, we find only one—the conclusion-indicator word *so*, which occurs in the last sentence of paragraph 4. The statement that *so* introduces is indeed the conclusion of the argument: "So the Design Argument alone cannot prove that the Theists' God rather than some other type of God or gods exists." This sentence, however, is a reiteration of the conclusion, which is also stated (in different words) for the first time in paragraph 2: "[The design argument] doesn't prove the existence of a unique, all-powerful, all-knowing, and all-good God."

After identifying the conclusion, we can see that the first premise must be in paragraph 3: "Even if you accept that the world and everything in it clearly shows evidence of having been designed, there is no reason to believe that it was all designed by one God." Perhaps the world was designed by many gods. The design argument gives us no reason to rule out this possibility.

The second premise, then, is in paragraph 4: "the [design] argument doesn't necessarily support the view that the Designer (or designers) was all-powerful." Perhaps the designer was weak, or inexperienced, or mortal. The design argument doesn't prove otherwise.

When we outline the argument, we get this:

Premise 1 • Even if you accept that the world and everything in it clearly shows evidence of having been designed, there is no reason to believe that it was designed by one God.

Premise 2 • The [design] argument doesn't necessarily support the view that the Designer (or designers) was all-powerful.

Conclusion • So the design argument alone cannot prove that the Theists' God rather than some other type of God or gods exist.

For the sake of clarity, we can paraphrase the argument:

Premise 1 • The design argument doesn't show that the world must have been created by just one God.

Premise 2 • The design argument doesn't show that the world must have been created by an all powerful God.

Conclusion • Therefore, the design argument doesn't show that an all-powerful, all-knowing, and all-good God exists rather some other type of God or gods.

Now we ask the crucial question mandated by *Rule 2-2*: does the conclusion follow from the premises? In this case, we would have to say yes. If the design argument fails to show that the creator is one God, and if it fails to show that the creator is all-powerful, then we must conclude that the design argument fails to show that the Judeo-Christian or Islamic version of God exists. That is, the author's argument is valid.

Next we ask the question prompted by *Rule 2-3*: are the premises true? More carefully, does our evidence make it reasonable for us to think they are true? In some cases, what is reasonable for you to believe to be true is reasonable for me to believe to be false—but then one of us must have a false belief. By studying the excerpt, most of us will see that the design argument, if cogent, supports only the claim that the world had a designer (or designers). The argument does not show, however, that the designer had any distinguishing characteristics, including attributes associated with the notion of God in the major monotheistic religions. If this is the case, then we should think *Premise 1* is true—for all the design argument shows, any supposed designer could have been one or many. Likewise, we should think *Premise 2* is true—for all the design argument shows, any supposed designer could have been less than all-powerful.

Based on this analysis, we should judge that the author's argument is sound—that is, it is valid and we find all of its premises reasonable to accept. It is a strong argument for us. The design argument—in the form presented in our excerpt—does not prove the existence of the God from monotheistic traditions. Our analysis, however, is not the final word on the topic. We have not considered certain other arguments relevant to the issues raised.

---

## ❧ QUICK REVIEW ❧
### Basic Definitions

- **Statement (declarative sentence)**
  An assertion that something is or is not the case. A statement expresses a proposition.

- **Proposition**
  The "meaning" of a statement—it is either true or false (and not both). Different statements can express the same proposition.

- **Argument**
  A combination of statements, some of which are intended to support another of them. Statements supposedly providing the support are the premises; the statement supposedly being supported is the conclusion.

- **Deductive argument**
  An argument intended to offer logically conclusive support for its conclusion. It could be valid or invalid.

- **Inductive argument**
  An argument intended to offer support for its conclusion, but whose premises are not intended to guarantee the conclusion's truth. It could be cogent or ill-formed.

- **Valid argument**
  An argument that has a form such that if its premises were true, its conclusion would be, too.

- **Invalid argument**
  An argument that is not valid. Some of these are ill-formed, some are cogent.

- **Cogent argument**
  An argument whose premises, if true, would support its conclusion without it being the case that if the premises are true, the conclusion must be true.

- **Ill-formed argument**
  An argument that has a form such that its premises, even if they were true, would provide no support for its conclusion. It is neither valid nor cogent.

- **Well-formed argument**
  An argument that is either valid or cogent.

- **Sound argument**
  A valid argument with all true premises. (There is no agreed-upon term for a cogent argument with all true premises.)

- **Strong argument**
  This concept is relativized to a person. A strong argument for person *x* is one that rationally compels person *x* to accept its conclusion. That is, it is well-formed *and* it has premises all of which are reasonable for person *x* to accept. Furthermore, in the case of cogent arguments, the argument is not overturned by other statements reasonable for person *x* to accept.

- **Weak argument**
  This concept, too, is relativized to a person, as it refers to an argument that is not strong.

## For discussion:

- Can a proposition be true and false at the same time? Why or why not?
- If I say, "I like broccoli," and you say, "I dislike broccoli," do we disagree?
- Is it the case that every proposition that you have good reason to think is true, is, in fact, true?
- What does it really mean to say that a proposition is true?
- Can you give an example of a proposition that you currently believe but that is false?

- Can you give an example of a proposition that you previously believed to be true but that is actually false?
- Are all ill-formed arguments invalid? Are all invalid arguments ill-formed?
- Is every sound argument strong for you? Why or why not?
- How could a cogent argument with all and only premises you find reasonable to accept not be strong for you?

# Notes

1.  In our discussion here, we are not always careful to distinguish statements from propositions, but this should not cause any serious problems.

2.  Cogency is not a formal (i.e., structural) matter in the way that validity is. For the sake of this example, it is important to assume that an arbitrary person has only a small, insufficiently representative sample. For more nuanced discussion, consider a philosophy of science or critical thinking course.

3.  Terminology here varies significantly. In fact, the definitions in this edition are different from those in the first, partly to allow for sensible discussion of the difference between a proposition being true and it being rational for a person to think that it is. (You might find looking at the questions for further discussion at the end of this chapter enlightening.) Follow your instructor's lead and, if you encounter such terms as *strong*, *ill-formed*, *cogent*, and *sound* in other contexts, be sure you understand their meaning there.

4.  A fuller discussion of induction (which is outside the scope of this book) would elaborate on the concept of "defeaters" for inductive arguments. They are propositions that, if rationally believed to be true, would overturn rational acceptance of an otherwise inductively strong argument. There is no analogous concept for valid arguments.

5.  Excerpted from Chapter 1 of Nigel Warburton, *Philosophy: The Basics* (London: Routledge, 2000), 12, 14–15. Reproduced by permission of the publisher.

# ❧ 3 ❧
# Rules of Style and Content for Philosophical Writing

Fortunately, there is much in the craft of essay writing that is the same no matter what your subject or purpose. To a comforting degree, writing is writing. There are matters of composition, grammar, punctuation, and usage (topics covered in Chapters 8 and 9) relevant to any kind of essay you write.

Nonetheless, some features of philosophical writing are distinctive—or, as you may be tempted to say, peculiar. Some are characteristic of the genre, and others just take on more importance. These features concern both content (what is said) and form (how it is said), and you must know how to handle them all if you are to write good philosophy essays.

For guidance, consider the following rules—and through practice learn how to apply them competently.

## Rule 3-1   Write to Your Audience

Almost everything you write—from university papers to love notes—is intended for a particular audience. Knowing who your audience is can make all the difference in what you say and how you say it. Unless things have gone terribly awry, you would not ordinarily address members of town council the same way you would your one true love, nor your one true love as you would readers of the *Globe and Mail*. You may wonder, then, who the intended audience of your philosophy paper is.

Your instructor, of course, may specify your audience and thus settle the issue for you. Otherwise, you should assume that your audience consists of intelligent, curious readers who know little about philosophy but who are capable of understanding and appreciating a clearly written, well-made paper on any variety of subjects, including philosophy. Unless you have instructions to the contrary, you should *not* assume that your audience consists of your instructor, professional philosophers generally, philosophy students who know more than you do, or readers who will either agree with everything you say or reject your thesis out of hand. Writing to your proper audience as outlined here means that you will need to define unfamiliar terms, explain any points that may be misunderstood, and lay out your argument so that its structure and significance would be clear to any intelligent reader. This approach will both force you to attempt a better understanding of your subject and help you to demonstrate this understanding through your writing.

If you know more about your readers than this general description would suggest, then you can tailor your essay to them. How much do your readers know about the issue? Are they adamantly opposed to your position? Are they mostly in agreement with you? How important is the issue to them? What common interests do you share with them? Do you hope that your essay will change people's minds or just help them better appreciate or tolerate your view? Knowing the answers to any of these questions could change how you present your case.

### Rule 3-2   Avoid Pretentiousness

Philosophy is profound, highbrow, and lofty; therefore, you should try to make your philosophy paper sound profound, highbrow, and lofty. Do you believe this? Some people who are new to philosophy do. They think that philosophical writing is supposed to sound grand, as if it were meant for God himself—or God's exalted servant, their philosophy instructor. This view is mistaken.

Good philosophy is often profound, but the profundity comes from the ideas or arguments expressed—not from fancy, overblown writing. Writing that tries merely to *seem* grand is pretentious, and pretentious writing is bad writing whether composed by philosophers or philosophy students. (Alas, some philosophical writing is pretentious, even when the ideas presented are worthy of consideration, so you cannot always take assigned readings as exemplars of unpretentiousness. Plus, styles change—what is pretentious now might merely have been polite earlier.)

Pretentious writing is bad, in part, because it is empty. Like a pastry punctured by a fork, pretentious writing collapses when closely examined, proving that the outside is puffy while the inside has little substance. Philosophy papers are supposed to offer real arguments in support of a worthwhile conclusion. Intelligent readers (especially instructors) are likely to get impatient with pretentious language that tries to cover up a lack of argument or insight. It is far better to concentrate on presenting a good argument in plain, clear language.

Consider this passage:

> Indubitably, the question as to whether utilitarianism can, through the utilization of a consideration of parameters that effectuate the amplification of life, liberty, and the pursuit of happiness for all who live and breathe in this earthly realm, enhance human happiness is of paramount importance.

This is pretentiousness gone wild, the cause of which is in plain sight. First, we meet several fancy words (with three to five syllables) that can be eliminated or replaced with simpler terms   *indubitably, utilization, parameters, effectuate, amplification,* and *paramount.* Second, the passage contains some unnecessarily ornate or lengthy phrases (some of which are also clichés)—*the question as to whether; life, liberty, and the pursuit of happiness;* and *all who live and breathe in this earthly realm.* Third, the passage as a whole is pointlessly complex, an annoying problem that partially conceals the ordinariness of the passage's meaning.

Look at this version:

> Whether utilitarian principles can enhance human happiness is an important question.

We have gone from a sprawling, bombastic passage to a single, plain sentence without a significant loss in meaning. The new version is better. It is clear and straightforward—and does not pretend to be something it's not. (See Chapter 8 for related discussions on writing effective sentences.)

### Rule 3-3    Keep the Authority of Philosophers in Perspective

In Chapter 7 we delve into the documentation of philosophy papers. This rule, however, addresses a related but separate issue: how to use the authority of philosophers in your papers.

As we have seen, using evidence, including the testimony of experts, is a legitimate way to support premises or conclusions in arguments, including arguments put forth in philosophy papers. You must be careful, however, when you try to back up your arguments by citing a philosopher. Remember that in philosophy, the world turns on arguments. Propositions and positions are advanced and challenged, accepted and rejected, based on the worth of relevant arguments. In a philosophical essay, the argument matters most, and the essential questions are whether the conclusion follows from the premises and whether the premises are true. Thus, if a philosopher—even a famous one—carries any weight in your essay, it is only because of his or her arguments. The mere fact that the philosopher is recognized as an authority (or is famous, reputable, or popular) cannot, by itself, have any bearing on whether a proposition is worthy of acceptance. So if you want to prove that all persons have free will, merely showing that this is the belief of a noted philosopher cannot bolster your case one bit. Citing a good argument devised by the philosopher, however, can strengthen your case—because the argument is good, not because it comes from a particular author. (As explained in Chapter 7, the source of any such reference, of course, must be properly documented.)

### Rule 3-4    Do Not Overstate Premises or Conclusions

Overstatement is the problem of exaggerating claims, of bestowing an assertion with a stronger or more inclusive sound than it deserves. We are all guilty of overstatement, most often in everyday speech. We may say, "Everyone dislikes Professor Jones," or "Americans think the French are snobbish," when in fact only *some* students dislike Professor Jones and only *a few* of our American friends think that *some* French people are snobbish. In everyday conversation, such exaggerations are often understood as such and are used innocuously for emphasis. But too often overstatements are simply distortions, assertions that claim too much and lead us into error or prejudice. To a disconcerting degree, assertions regarding opposing views in religion, politics, and morality are overstatements. (See Chapter 6, especially the discussions of the fallacies known as *hasty generalization, slippery slope,* and *straw man.*)

In philosophical essays, overstatement is never acceptable, and you must be on your guard against it. It raises doubts in your readers' minds about your judgment, your truthfulness, and your arguments. Even one overblown adjective or a single over-the-top phrase can undermine your credibility. Overstatement leads readers to think, "Here is an exaggeration; what else in this essay is exaggerated?"

In philosophical writing, overstatement arises in two ways. First, particular statements—including premises—can be exaggerated. You may be tempted to assert that whatever issue you are addressing in your essay is "the most important issue of our time." You might declare that a premise is certainly or undoubtedly true (when in fact it is merely probable) or forgo important qualifiers such as "some," "perhaps," and "many." You may get carried away and say, for example, that killing another human being is *always* morally wrong, even though you might admit that killing in self-defence is morally permissible.

Second, the conclusions of arguments can be overstated: they can go beyond what logical inference would permit. As we saw in the previous chapter, a conclusion must follow from its premises. Because of your commitment to your conclusion, however, you may overstate it. The result is an invalid or weak argument.

## Rule 3-5    Do Not Rely on Rhetorical Questions

A (merely) rhetorical question is a question that the reader is supposed to answer a certain way. It is, in effect, a disguised declarative sentence. For example:

Isn't it obvious that computers cannot think?

How could anyone doubt that genetically modified organisms are dangerous?

Have we ever faced a greater problem than climate change?

The idea is for the reader to turn these questions into declarative sentences by answering them in the way the author hopes. (For example, "Yes, it's obvious that computers cannot think.") Asking such a "question" is not a substitute for providing an argument for the relevant claim. (See also *begging the question* in Chapter 6.)

## Rule 3-6    Treat Opponents and Opposing Views Fairly

Sometimes it seems that most of what people believe about arguing for a position has been learned from an unreliable source—political debate-type television programs, for example. In these forums, the standard procedure is to attack the character and motivations of opponents, distort or misrepresent opposing views, and dismiss opponents' evidence and concerns out of hand. This approach is neither condoned nor tolerated in philosophical writing. As we have seen, the ideal in philosophical discourse is the disinterested and fair-minded search for truth among all parties. Abusive or unfair tactics are out of order. They are also ineffective. When readers encounter such heavy-handedness, they are likely to be suspicious of the writer's motives, to question whether his or her assertions can be trusted, or to doubt the worth of arguments defended with such gratuitous zeal.

There are two common sources of unfairness in your papers (both are discussed further in Chapter 6):

1.  The straw man fallacy
2.  The ad hominem fallacy

The **straw man fallacy** consists of the distorting, weakening, or oversimplifying of someone's position so it can be more easily attacked or refuted. For example:

> Greenpeace is opposed to whaling because they want to force every human to be vegan—to subsist without consuming any animal products at all. They want the International Court of Justice to forbid fishing of any sort by anybody anywhere.

Here, Greenpeace and its views on whaling are mischaracterized to make them seem ridiculous and easy to argue against. It is doubtful that Greenpeace (or any other organization) wants to *force* people to have certain dietary customs. Likewise, the description of Greenpeace's views in the second sentence is inaccurate. Even most pro-whaling groups would not characterize Greenpeace's stand in such a misleading way.

The point is that opposing views and arguments should be described fairly and accurately, acknowledging any strengths they have. This approach is likely to result in (1) your readers viewing you as more honest and conscientious, and (2) your trying to find ways to address any weaknesses exposed in your own argument.

The **ad hominem fallacy** (also known as *appeal to* or *attack on the person fallacy*) consists of rejecting a claim on the grounds that there is something wrong not with the claim but with the person who makes it. Consider the following:

You can't believe anything Jan says about the existence of souls. She's a philosophy major.

We should reject the arguments put forth by the so-called great thinkers who think that there is such a thing as the rights of persons. Who cares what they think?

These "arguments" are baseless because they try to refute or undermine a claim by appealing to a person's character or motives. But a person's character or motives almost never have any bearing on a claim's worth. Claims must be judged by the reasons they have, or do not have, in their favour.

## Rule 3-7   Write Clearly

Being clear is a matter of ensuring that your meaning is understood by the reader. Clarity in philosophical prose is arguably more important than in most other types of non-fiction because philosophy deals with so many difficult and unfamiliar ideas.

Lack of clarity in your writing can occur in several ways. Inexperienced writers often produce murky papers because they assume that if they know what they mean, others will know too. Typically, others do *not* know. The problem is that new writers have not yet developed the knack of viewing their own writing as others might. In other words, they fail to adopt an objective stance toward their own words. Good writers are their own best critics.

Trying to view your writing as others might takes practice. One helpful tactic is not to look at your writing for a day or two, then to go back to it and read it cold. You may discover after you take this little break that some passages, which earlier seemed clear, are mostly gibberish.

Another technique is to use peer review. Ask a friend to read your paper and pinpoint any unclear passages. Your friend doesn't have to know anything about philosophy. He or she just needs to be like your target audience—intelligent, curious, and able to appreciate what you're trying to do. (If you get any ideas from your friend [or elsewhere!], be sure to cite appropriately; see Chapter 7.)

Ambiguity renders writing less clear. A statement is problematically ambiguous if it has more than one meaning and the context doesn't help clear things up. (See also Chapter 6 for the fallacy of equivocation, in which ambiguity is exploited to give the appearance of a valid argument.)

Some ambiguities are *semantic*: they are the result of multiple meanings of a word or phrase. Consider the sentence "Kids make nutritious snacks." The word *make* could mean *prepare* or *constitute*. If the former, the sentence says that kids prepare good food. If the latter, the sentence means that kids *are* good food. (There is a further ambiguity—do you see it?)

Some ambiguities are *syntactic*: they are the result of the way words are combined. Read this sentence straight through without pausing: "Maria saw the bird with binoculars." Who had the binoculars, Maria or the bird? We don't know because the sentence is poorly written; words are misplaced. If we want the sentence to say that Maria was the one holding the binoculars, we might rewrite it like this: "Using her binoculars, Maria saw the bird," or "Maria saw the bird through her binoculars" (though this latter sentence still leaves it open that the binoculars belong to the bird!). Context will usually disambiguate, but we need to be careful.

Often a lack of clarity comes not from ambiguous terms but from *vague* terms—words that fail to convey one definite meaning. This failure can be the result of many kinds of sloppiness but at the head of the list is the tendency to use words that are too *general*. General words refer to whole groups or classes of things, such as *soldiers*, *artists*, and *books*. Specific words, on the other hand, refer to more particular items, such as *Sam Steele*, *Emily Carr*, and *Never Cry Wolf*.

There is nothing inherently wrong with using general words; in fact, we *must* employ them. Used to excess, however, they muddy a philosophy paper. Consider these pairs:

1. (a) According to Hobbes, all persons are capable of free actions.

   (b) According to Hobbes, all persons are capable of free actions. A free action is one that is caused by someone's will and that is not constrained by another person or some physical force or barrier.

2. (a) In Kant's view of some aspects of human experience, there are conflicts between what moral considerations may lead us to conclude and acts in which one must aver a state of affairs that is contrary to fact.

   (b) Kant believes that lying is always immoral.

At first glance, sentence 1(a) may seem like a straightforward statement, but it is so general as to be almost mysterious. What is a *free action?* 1(b) is much more specific. It reiterates the first sentence but elaborates on it, stipulating two conditions that must be met before an action can be considered a free action. Notice that the general statement was made more specific by adding more information—information that narrowed down the countless possibilities.

In the second pair, 2(a) is packed with general terms, including *aspects of human experience, moral considerations,* and *acts in which one must aver a state of affairs that is contrary to fact.* This is an attempt to say what sentence 2(b) successfully communicates. Sentence 2(b) avoids as many generalities as possible and gets right to the point. The notion that lying is always immoral is, of course, a general principle, but there is much clarity to be gained by expressing it in more specific terms. Notice that in contrast to the first pair, the second pair of sentences obtained greater specificity by using fewer words, not more.

Writing a philosophy paper will always involve using general terms. The key is to make your writing as specific as your subject and purpose will allow. (See Chapters 8 and 9 for other ways to increase the clarity of your writing.)

## Rule 3-8    Avoid Inappropriate Emotional Appeals

Emotional appeals in philosophical writing are almost always inappropriate and are usually considered elementary errors. Probably the worst offence is the substitution of emotion for arguments or premises. This ploy is a fallacy called, not surprisingly, *appeal to emotion:* the attempt to persuade someone of a conclusion not by offering a good argument but by trying to arouse the reader's feelings of fear, guilt, pity, anger, and the like. For example:

> Ladies and gentlemen of the jury, you must find my client not guilty. He is the unfortunate result of grinding poverty, a mother who rejected him, and a legal system that does not care that he was once a ragged, orphaned child wandering the streets in search of a single kind heart.

The appeal here is to pity (see Chapter 6), and the passage is shot through with language designed to evoke it—*grinding poverty, a mother who rejected him,* and *ragged, orphaned child.* But note: no good reasons are offered for believing that the defendant is innocent. No logical support at all is provided for this conclusion. If such an appeal were intended as the lone argument in a philosophy paper, the paper would have to be judged a failure.

Now consider this piece of political rhetoric:

> Dear voters, if you elect my opponent to the highest office in the land, will house prices rise beyond the grasp of ordinary citizens? We, the taxpayers, cannot support further debt. Vote for fiscal responsibility. Vote for me.

This is a blatant appeal to fear (again, see Chapter 6), a common tactic in politics. No good reasons are provided, just a scary scenario. (Note, too, the use of a rhetorical question.)

Emotional appeals can seriously mislead the reader, even when they are not used as substitutes for arguments. By employing particular words or phrases that evoke strong emotions, a writer can powerfully influence the reader's attitudes and opinions. Look at the following:

> The anti-life forces in this country who favour abortion—the murder of a child simply because he or she exists—are no better than the Nazis, who also exterminated millions of people simply because they existed and were inconvenient to the state. The Machiavellian notion of abortion-on-demand should be replaced with the enlightened pro-life view that life is better than death.

This passage is emotionally revved up to provoke outrage and disgust—and the revving comes mostly from the use of a few powerfully evocative words. Word choice not only does most of the work, but also enhances the effect of some fallacies. Ponder *anti-life, murder of a child, Nazis, exterminated millions, Machiavellian,* and *enlightened.* All these words are used misleadingly—and persuasively. Most of them form part of a straw man argument, while some add teeth to an appeal to the person attack. Although the majority of emotive words are designed to cast abortion and abortion-rights advocates in a bad light, the term *enlightened* is used to evoke positive feelings about the pro-life side.

---

### Five Common Mistakes in Philosophical Writing

1. Covering up a poor argument or lack of understanding with pretentious language.
2. Overstating your case or begging the question.
3. Ridiculing opponents or opposing views.

4. Being guilty of the straw man or the appeal to the person fallacy.
5. Using emotional appeals.

## Rule 3-9    Be Careful What You Assume

Behind every argument are presuppositions that need not be made explicit because they are taken for granted by all parties. They may be too obvious to mention or are in no need of justification. (They are distinct from implicit premises, which are essential to an argument and should be brought out into the open.) In arguments about the rights of hospital patients, for example, there would typically be no need to explain that a hospital is not a Chevrolet truck, or that patient rights have something to do with ethics, or that such rights may be important to patients. You should, however, be careful not to presuppose a claim that may be controversial among your readers. If you wish to establish that abortion is morally permissible, you should not assume your readers will agree that women have a right to choose abortion or that a fetus is not a person.

## Rule 3-10    Write in First Person

Unless your instructor tells you otherwise, use first person singular pronouns (I, me, my, mine) rather than the more formal we ("We will show that . . .") or extremely formal and stilted passive locutions such as "It is to be noted that . . ." or "It is to be shown that. . . ." This advice correlates nicely with using the active voice (*Rule 9-2*) and taking full responsibility for the claims you make ("I contend that . . .").

## Rule 3-11    Avoid Discriminatory Language

Sexist or racist language implies that a particular group of people is somehow not as good as other groups. This prejudicial way of speaking or writing can sneak into prose in several ways. Sometimes it happens when people refer to a group as if it were not really part of society as a whole. Here is one explanation of the problem:

> Some common ways of speaking and writing, for example, assume that "normal" people are all white males. It is still common practice, for instance, to mention a person's race, gender, or ethnic background

if the person is not a white male, and not to do so if the person is. Thus, if we are talking about a white male from Ontario, we are apt to say simply, "He is from Ontario." But if the male is, say, Cree, we might tend to mention that fact and say, "He is a Cree from Ontario"—even when the person's ethnic background is irrelevant to whatever we are talking about. This practice assumes that the "normal" person is not Cree and by implication insinuates that if you are, then you are "different" and a deviation from the norm, an outsider.

Of course, it may be relevant to your topic that this particular man is a Cree from Ontario; if so, there is absolutely nothing wrong with writing "He is a Cree from Ontario."[1]

Unfortunately, some discriminatory tendencies are built into the English language. Traditionally, masculine pronouns have been used to refer to individuals even though they could be either male or female. For example:

A good scientist will always check *his* work.

Any CEO of a large corporation will work hard because *he* is conscientious.

Usually, the best remedy is either to use *both* masculine and feminine pronouns or to switch to the plural:

A good scientist will always check *his or her* work.
Good scientists will always check *their* work.

Any CEO of a large corporation will work hard because *he or she* is conscientious.
CEOs of large corporations will work hard because *they* are conscientious.

If this approach doesn't eliminate discriminatory wording, you may have to overhaul the whole sentence:

Scientific work should always be checked.
Conscientious CEOs of large corporations work hard.

## Rules of Style and Content

Rule 3-1: Write to your audience.
Rule 3-2: Avoid pretentiousness.
Rule 3-3: Keep the authority of philosophers in perspective.
Rule 3-4: Do not overstate premises or conclusions.
Rule 3-5: Do not rely on rhetorical questions.
Rule 3-6: Treat opponents and opposing views fairly.
Rule 3-7: Write clearly.
Rule 3-8: Avoid inappropriate emotional appeals.
Rule 3-9: Be careful what you assume.
Rule 3-10: Write in first person.
Rule 3-11: Avoid discriminatory language.

*For further information:*

- There are many good books on writing. A standard is *The Elements of Style* [various editions], by William Strunk, Jr., and E.B. White (Longman/Pearson). It is a very practical reference guide.

- An entertaining and more recent book is Stanley Fish's *How to Write a Sentence: And How to Read One* (HarperCollins, 2011). Offering many literary examples, this book is perhaps best suited to those truly curious about the expressive power of English, as opposed to those looking for a reference work.

# Note

1.    Adapted from Brooke Noel Moore and Richard Parker, *Critical Thinking*, 6th ed. (Mountain View: Mayfield Publishing, 2001), 71.

# ❧ 4 ❧
# Exegetical and Expository Writing

Most philosophy essays involve asserting and defending a thesis (see Chapter 5). But not all do, and even those that do usually involve an element of the topic of this chapter—exegetical and expository writing.

An **exegesis** is a careful interpretation or analysis of a written work. Historically, the term *exegesis* was reserved for the analysis and interpretation of religious texts, but its meaning has been expanded to include any scholarly writing—ancient or contemporary, religious or not. An **exposition** is a description or explanation of (in this context) a philosophical position, theory, or idea. Since much of philosophy is, in effect, writing in response to the writings of other philosophers, exegesis and exposition are closely linked.

You might be assigned explicitly the task of writing an entire essay describing an author's view, interpreting the meaning of a passage, or characterizing a theory. Or you might find yourself needing to explain a position or a quotation in the context of writing an argumentative essay, where your ultimate goal is defending a thesis. At any rate, if a significant degree of detail or rigour is expected, you will need to go beyond mere paraphrase or summary. (See Chapter 7 for more on quoting, paraphrasing, and summarizing, and Appendix B for how to document your sources properly.)

Questions to consider when writing an exegetical or expository essay include the following: What precise passages in a work indicate that the author holds the view that you attribute? How does this work relate to other works by the same author? How does the author's view fit with other (especially other plausible) views? What is a differing view, especially one from which proponents of the position in question try to distance themselves? (Any contrast can be very instructive in interpreting the author's meaning.) What alternative interpretations of the work are there, and why are they less plausible than the one you've chosen?

It is often important to reconstruct the overall problem facing the writer—what question was he or she trying to answer? To what end is the author going to put the view you ascribe? (What is the author's "overall game plan"?) Then you can describe how the author addresses the problem, and, sometimes, why the author chooses one answer over another, or phrases things a particular way. Setting the discussion in context can make things clearer for both you and your reader.

In any event, writing an exegetical or expository essay (or part of an essay) involves defending your position—why should the reader think that your interpretation or explanation is correct? At the risk of making things needlessly confusing, it might be useful to say that often such an essay *is* an argumentative essay with the implicit thesis being that your interpretation or explanation is the right one or, at least, a very reasonable or interesting one.

## Rule 4-1   Be Charitable When Characterizing the Views of Others

Before you can begin a piece of exegetical or expository writing, you must read what you are going to interpret, analyze, or explain. We hope this strikes you as obvious, but mentioning it allows us to remind you to check back to Chapter 1 on how to read philosophy—slowly, carefully, actively, and critically.

It is important to be in the right frame of mind when approaching a written work. This goes for all fields, not just philosophy. You should not read a work from the point of view of a fawning admirer with no critical thoughts at all. Just because something is in print doesn't mean it's true. (Honest!) But you should not read a work as a naysayer bent on showing the author's view to be ludicrous. Either one of these extremes can be especially tempting when you intend the result of your investigation to form the backdrop for an essay arguing for or against the view you characterize.

So, start by being charitable. If you think that two interpretations are equally possible based on the text, give the author the benefit of the doubt and attribute the more plausible of the two. Adopting this degree of sympathy for the author will not make you unable to be critical—it will simply render the view you attribute more likely to be the one the author holds and also more likely to be worthy of examination (recall *Rule 3-5*).

Even if you are leaning toward the fawning admirer end of the spectrum, this rule should help since it should encourage you to look for even more plausible alternatives to the view you favour; it also requires you to adopt the same charitable attitude to the works of those who disagree.

### Rule 4-2    Provide Evidence That Your Interpretation Is Correct

Your reader should be forgiven for not taking your word that the author is saying what you suggest she or he is saying. Evidence is in order. Almost always this will involve direct quotations: what exact sequence of words is part of what makes you think that the author holds the view you attribute to him or her? (**Important:** refer to Chapter 7 for help in learning to quote, paraphrase, and summarize effectively, and Appendix B for how to cite sources properly.)

Let's look at an example:

> Neander thinks that natural selection is not merely a negative force, culling variants that are less worthy. Rather, she argues that, while it plays a role in explaining the persistence of traits in populations, selection also plays a role in explaining the occurrence of those traits in current particular individuals. She writes that selection "not only explains the fact that virtually all humans have opposable thumbs, it also explains (in part) how it is that you and I have opposable thumbs."[1]

Of course, at this point, a lot of work still remains, whatever the topic of the essay in which this paragraph were to occur. What are the details of the author's view and why does she think what she does? To what use is this exegesis going to be put? But at least the reader has reason to think the paper is starting off on the right track. More textual evidence could be brought in later as required.

Providing textual support is especially important for any aspects of your interpretation that could be considered contentious. What claims that you attribute to the author are such that the average person would need to be persuaded that they are true, and hence persuaded that the author believes them to be true? For instance, you would probably require almost no evidence for the claim that your instructor thinks that Canada is in North America, but rather a lot for the claim that your instructor thinks the Earth is flat!

In university courses, there is often an expectation that students demonstrate familiarity with (at least some of) the assigned reading by showing its relevance to what they have to say. Aside from demonstrating due diligence with respect to the readings, referring to class material can help keep a paper grounded and on topic. So, tie your interpretation explicitly to the text, especially when it comes to matters under dispute. It is quite unlikely that a good exegesis or exposition would contain no quotations at all.

## Rule 4-3    Use Quotations Judiciously

This rule is not in conflict with *Rule 4-2*, though learning to apply them both takes some practice. The point is that a series of quotations is neither an exegesis nor an exposition. You cannot rely on texts to explain themselves; you need to paraphrase (again, see Chapter 7) and to make connections.

In any essay you write, the vast majority of its words should be your own. If you rely too heavily on quotations, it will seem as though you do not understand the works or issues you are considering well enough to be in a position to discuss them. Plus, you will not help to further the understanding of your reader, who may feel vaguely insulted or dismissed by your apparent lack of engagement.

One very useful concept here is that of a "quotation sandwich." You should provide, in your own words, some lead-in to a quotation, and then some follow-up on what you take the quotation to mean or its relevance to what you are discussing. In other words, the quotation should be properly "sandwiched" between remarks of your own. This is in contrast with the "hit and run quotation," which appears without warning and disappears just as quickly. You must make the relevance of any quotations you use clear; do not use them simply to pad your word count.[2]

## Rule 4-4    Draw on Context

In addition to quotations, evidence for your interpretation or understanding of a written piece could draw on what you take the overall project to be. What question is the author addressing? What else has the author written that bears on the subject? (Characterizing the author as inconsistent should be avoided if possible—an application of *Rule 4-1.*) Who are the author's interlocutors? What is the view (or what are the views) in opposition to the view you're considering? For example, the following passage discusses Descartes' purpose in beginning his "Meditations":

> Descartes begins his "Meditations" by outlining his decision to subject his beliefs to a very high standard of scrutiny, considering himself to have been lax in the past. In the First Meditation, he writes: "I will devote myself sincerely and without reservation to the demolition of my opinions."[3] That is, he will try to demonstrate to himself that he is not justified in believing much, if not all, of what he has believed to date. To help with the demolition, he invokes the possibility of a "malicious demon" who is all-powerful and is out to deceive him.[4] If there were such a demon (and Descartes, at this point, has no reason to think there is not), it seems Descartes could be wrong about almost everything. In the Second Meditation, he writes: "Anything which admits of the slightest doubt I will set aside just as if I had found it to be wholly false . . ."[5]

> From these passages, it might seem that Descartes is arguing in favour of skepticism. After all, readers are left with doubts they probably didn't have before. However, despite appearances, his appeals to doubt are not evidence that Descartes is a skeptic. He is not arguing that we have no reason to think our beliefs true; rather, he is attempting the "demolition" of his beliefs so that he can arrive at a set of true beliefs to which he is rationally entitled, with the hope that he can build from there. He sees the demolition as the first step in his quest "to establish anything at all in the sciences that [is] stable and likely to last."[6] In his reply to Hobbes, he writes that he introduced arguments against certainty "so that [he, Descartes] could reply to them in the subsequent Meditations."[7]

There is a limit to how much background, historical or philosophical, you can or should provide, but having the big picture in mind can be very helpful.

A related way to provide evidence that your interpretation is correct is to consider reasonable alternatives, then to give grounds for rejecting them. In the process of being charitable, you might have given serious consideration to a different interpretation. You might do well (but only if space and topic constraints permit!) to explain to the reader why you prefer the view you do. Does your view make more sense of the author's other writings? Does it answer the questions under consideration at this time? Does it answer current questions?

## Rule 4-5    If Appropriate, State Why the Issue Matters

Some essays devote a great deal of time and effort to unpacking a short but disputed passage, or to offering a concise and clear synopsis of a particular facet of a view. Writers of sophisticated essays of this sort usually follow *Rule 4-4* and situate the narrow issue in a wider philosophical or historical context. In short, they answer the questions: why should the reader be interested in this interpretation or idea? What follows from it? What follows from denying it? By following *Rule 4-4*, such writers wind up following *Rule 4-5*.

However, sometimes following *Rule 4-5* requires a more direct approach. Suppose there are two seemingly equally legitimate contenders when it comes to understanding a passage or explaining a view. Let your reader know this, then explain what hinges on a choice between them. Learning that interpretation *a* has the result *b*, and interpretation *c* has the result *d* could easily motivate interest in deciding between *a* and *c*. It could even tilt the balance if one of the results is far less plausible than the other.

If your exegesis or exposition is part of an argumentative essay, chances are good that the importance of your take on the view you've been discussing will become apparent when you appeal to it in your later discussion. This is not to say that you should not try to make it more salient for your readers, if space permits.

*For discussion:*

- Pick a passage in a work you are reading in class. Construct two possible interpretations of it. Which is more reasonable and why?
- Why should you be charitable in interpreting a writer's work or a particular passage?

*For further information:*

- Gerald Graff and Cathy Birkenstein, *"They Say / I Say": The Moves That Matter in Academic Writing*, 2nd ed. (New York: W.W. Norton & Co., 2009). This is a book on how to engage in the "conversation" of responding to the intellectual work of others.

# Notes

1. Karen Neander, "What Does Natural Selection Explain? Correction to Sober." *Philosophy of Science* 55(3) (September 1988): 422–426. The quotation is from 422–423.

2. The two concepts introduced in this paragraph ("quotation sandwich" and "hit and run quotation") come from Gerald Graff and Cathy Birkenstein, *"They Say / I Say": The Moves That Matter in Academic Writing*, 2nd ed. (New York: W.W. Norton & Co., 2009). Thanks to my colleague Holly Andersen for pointing me to this material.

3. Rene Descartes, "Meditations on First Philosophy" in *The Philosophical Writings of Descartes, Volume II*, trans. John Cottingham, Robert Stoothoff, and Dugald Murdoch (Cambridge: Cambridge University Press, 1641/1984), 12.

4. Ibid.

5. Ibid., 16.

6. Ibid., 12.

7. Rene Descartes, reply to "Third Set of Objections . . .". Ibid., 12.

# ❧ 5 ❧
# Defending a Thesis in an Argumentative Essay

In conversations, letters to the editor, or online discussions, have you ever taken a position on an issue and offered reasons why your view is correct? If so, you have *defended a thesis*. You have presented an argument, giving reasons for accepting a particular thesis or conclusion. If you elaborate on your argument in a written paper, you create something even more valuable—a *argumentative* (or *thesis defence*) *essay*.

In an **argumentative essay**, you try to show the reader that your view is worthy of acceptance by offering reasons that support it. Your thesis may assert your position on a philosophical, social, or political issue; or on the arguments or claims of other writers (including some famous or not-so-famous philosophers); or, really, on any issue at all. In every case, you affirm a thesis and give reasons for your affirmation.

This type of essay is not merely an analysis of claims, or a summary of points made by someone else, or a reiteration of what other people believe or say—although a good argumentative essay may contain these elements. (See Chapter 4 on exegetical and expository writing.) An argumentative essay is supposed to be a demonstration of what *you* believe and *why* you believe it. What other people think is, ultimately, beside the point.

For many students, this kind of writing seems like unknown terrain. This land can be traversed only by thinking things through and by understanding claims and the reasons behind them—and newer students may not be accustomed to such a trip. The journey, however, turns out to be worthwhile and contains elements that are familiar from advertising, political speeches, newspaper editorials, and so on. Much of the world's work gets done by defending a thesis, whether it's in the context of special interest advocacy, legal casework, business communication, a press release, or a piece of academic work. Success or failure depends on your ability to make your own case in writing or to evaluate cases that come your way.

## Basic Argumentative Essay Structure

Argumentative essays usually contain the following elements, although not necessarily in this order:

    I.  Introduction (or opening)
       a) Thesis statement (the claim to be supported)
       b) Plan for the paper
       c) Background for the thesis
    II.  Argument supporting the thesis
    III.  Assessment of objections
    IV.  Conclusion

### Introduction

The introduction may be only the paper's first paragraph, sometimes just a sentence or two. Occasionally it stretches to several paragraphs. The length depends on how much ground you must cover to introduce the argument. Whatever the length, the introduction should be no longer than necessary. In most cases the best introductions are short.

If a rule of thumb exists for what the introduction must contain, it is this: the introduction should set forth the **thesis statement**. The thesis statement usually appears in the first paragraph. It is the claim that you hope to support or prove in your essay, the conclusion of the argument that you intend to present. You may want to pose the thesis statement as the answer to a question that you raise or as the solution to a problem that you wish to discuss. However presented, your thesis statement is the assertion you must support with reasons. It serves as a compass to your readers, guiding them from paragraph to paragraph, premise to premise, showing them a clear path from introduction to conclusion. It also helps *you* stay on course. It reminds you to relate every sentence and paragraph to your one controlling idea.

In some argumentative essays—many newspaper editorials and magazine articles, for example—the thesis statement is not stated but is implied, just as in some arguments the premises or even the conclusion is implied. In philosophical writing, however, the thesis should always be explicit, asserted plainly in a carefully crafted sentence. Most likely, in any argumentative essay you write in university, you will be expected to include a thesis statement.

Your thesis statement should be restricted to a claim that you can defend in the space allowed. You want to state it in a single sentence and do so as early as possible. (More on how to devise a properly restricted thesis statement in a moment.) You may need to add a few words to explain or elaborate on the statement if you think its meaning or implications are unclear.

## ❦ How Not to Begin Your Philosophy Paper ❦

No offence intended, but student philosophy papers often begin poorly. They may open with a cliché, an irrelevant comment, an obvious or superfluous observation, or a long-winded lead-in to the thesis statement. Here are some examples:

- "Bertrand Russell [or some other philosopher] wrote many books."
- "From the beginning of time, people have wondered about . . ."
- "This paper will examine the ridiculous ideas of the atheist Jean-Paul Sartre."
- "The Bible tells us that . . ."
- "According to the *Canadian Oxford Dictionary*, the word *necessity* means . . ."
- "As everyone knows, humans have free will . . ."

The other two parts of an introduction—the **plan** for the paper and **background information** for the thesis—may or may not be necessary, depending on your thesis and your intent. In more formal essays, you will need not only to state your thesis but also to spell out how you intend to argue for it. You will need to summarize your whole argument—each of your premises and conclusion—or, if your argument is too long or complex, to summarize at least the most important points. Providing background information for your thesis is a matter of explaining what your thesis means (which includes defining terms and clarifying concepts), what its implications are, and sometimes why the issue is important. Sometimes the needed background information is so extensive that you must supply much of it after the introduction. At any rate, by adding the right kind of background information, you give your readers good reason to care about what you are saying and to continue reading.

In many philosophy papers, the background information includes a summary or sketch of the views of other philosophers (see Chapter 4). This can help to situate and motivate your position, partly by helping the reader understand why your topic is worth exploring and why your argument is relevant.

## Argument Supporting the Thesis

Between your paper's introduction and conclusion is the **body** of the essay. The basic components of the body are (1) the premises of your argument plus the material that supports or explains them and (2) an evaluation of objections to your thesis. Each premise must be clearly stated, carefully explained and illustrated, and properly backed up by examples, statistics, expert opinion, argument, or other reasons or evidence. You may be able to adequately develop the essay by devoting a single paragraph to each premise, or you may have to use several paragraphs per premise.

Whatever approach you take, you must stick to the central rule of paragraph development: develop just one main point in each paragraph, embodying that point in a topic sentence. Make sure that each paragraph in turn relates to your thesis statement.

If your essay is a critique of someone else's arguments, you should examine them in the body, explaining how they work and laying out the author's response to any major criticisms of them. Your account of the arguments should be accurate and complete, putting forth the author's best case and providing enough detail for your readers to understand the import of your own argument. (Again, see Chapter 4.) After the presentation of the author's side of things, you can then bring in your critique, asserting and explaining each premise.

Some premises, of course, may be so obvious that they do not require support. The determining factor is whether your readers would be likely to question them. If your readers are likely to accept a premise as it is, no backup is required. If they are not, you need to support the premise. A common mistake is to assume that a premise would be accepted by everyone when in fact it is controversial (*Rule 3-9*).

In any case, you should present only your strongest premises. One weak premise can spoil the whole argument. To the reader, one flimsy premise is a reason to be suspicious of all the rest. It is better to include one good premise that you can support than five bad premises that are unsupportable.

Recall that in a good argument the conclusion logically follows from the premises, and the premises are acceptable to the reader. Your task in the body of your essay is to put forth such an argument and to do so plainly—to clearly demonstrate to your readers that your premises are properly related to your conclusion and that they should be accepted as true. You should leave no doubt about what you are trying to prove and how you are trying to prove it. In longer papers, you may want to back up your thesis with more than one argument. This is an acceptable way to proceed, provided you make the relationships between the separate arguments and your thesis clear.

## Assessment of Objections

Often, an argumentative essay includes an assessment of objections— a sincere effort to take into account any objections or doubts that readers are likely to have about your points. In this case, you must show your readers that the objections are unfounded, that your argument is not fatally wounded by likely criticisms. Contrary to what some may think, when you deal effectively with objections in your essay you do not weaken it—you strengthen it. You earn credibility by making an attempt to be fair and thorough. You bolster your position by removing doubts from your readers' minds. If you don't confront likely objections, your readers may conclude either that you are ignorant of the objections or that you don't have a good reply to them. An extra benefit is that in dealing with objections, you may see ways to make your argument stronger.

On the other hand, you may discover that you do not have an adequate answer to the objections. Then what? Then you look for ways to change your arguments or thesis to overcome the criticisms. You can deliberately weaken your thesis by making it less sweeping or by acknowledging uncertainty, though take care not to "sit on the fence"— your thesis must still be clear and you must defend it. Alternatively, you may need to abandon your thesis altogether in favour of one that is more defensible. Discovering that your beloved thesis is full of holes is not necessarily a setback; you have increased your understanding by finding out which boats will float and which will not.

You should not consider every possible objection, just the strongest ones. You might use objections that you have encountered in your reading and research, or heard from others, or just dreamed up on your own. (See Chapter 7 for how to cite these sources appropriately!) Whatever you do, do not select pseudo-objections—those that you know are weak and easily demolished. Careful readers (including your instructor!) will see through this game and will think less of your paper.

Where in your paper you bring up objections can vary. You may choose to deal with objections as you go along—as you present each of your premises. On the other hand, you may want to handle objections at the beginning of the essay or near the end after defending the premises.

## Conclusion

Unless your essay is very short, it should have a **conclusion**, usually appearing in the last paragraph. Many conclusions reiterate the thesis statement and then go on to emphasize how important it is. Others issue a call to action, present a compelling perspective on the issue, or discuss further implications of the thesis statement. Some conclusions contain a summary of the essay's argument. A summary is always a good idea if the argument is complex, long, or formal.

# A Well-Built Essay

How might all of these parts fit together to make an essay? To find out, read the brief paper by Kathleen Moore[1] and review the comments that follow. You will see that although it is short and structurally simple, it has all the major elements that longer and more complex essays do. (There are no references to the paper's sources here, something that would normally be included in such an essay. We explore documentation styles in Chapter 7.)

The introduction of this essay is laid out in paragraphs 1 and 2. Paragraph 1 **introduces the topic**: the gap between rich and poor and whether the more affluent have a moral obligation to help narrow that gap. Background information includes the observation that the gap is wider than ever and that people all over the world are dying as a result of extreme poverty. These points impart a sense of urgency regarding the problem and help explain why the author thinks the issue matters and why the reader should care. The thesis statement is expressed in the last sentence of paragraph 1: "people who are relatively affluent should give a certain fair percentage of their earnings to help reduce absolute poverty on a global scale."

## Should Relatively Affluent People Help the Poor?

Kathleen Moore

1 As the world approaches the end of the twentieth century, the gap between rich and poor has never been wider. While some people have more money than it is possible to spend in a lifetime, no matter how lavishly they might make purchases, others are not able to provide even for their most basic needs. On all the continents of the world, people starve to death for lack of food, freeze to death for lack of shelter, die of diseases that could be prevented. The situation raises the issue of whether the affluent people of the world have a moral obligation to help the poor. I shall argue that people who are relatively affluent should give a certain fair percentage of their earnings to help reduce absolute poverty on a global scale.

2 My claim is that those who are relatively affluent, that is, people who would normally be defined as rich or wealthy in the context of a given society, have an obligation to give up a small but helpful percentage of their earnings. Peter Singer, an Australian philosopher, suggests ten percent. The money would be used to alleviate absolute poverty, a condition that Robert McNamara, the former president of the World Bank, defines as "characterized by malnutrition, illiteracy, disease, squalid

*Introduces topic, provides background.*

*Imparts a sense of urgency to issue.*

*Thesis statement.*

*Defines relevant terms.*

*Source is quoted.*

2

*Normally an endnote would go at end of this quotation.*

surroundings, high infant mortality and low life expectancy that is beneath any reasonable definition of human decency."

3 Many people argue that wealthy people should not have to help those who are needier than they, unless they choose to do so. The *Body of paper begins here.* strongest argument for this claim is articulated by Garrett Hardin, an ecologist from the University of Southern California. He points to the

*Writer paraphrases critic.*

harmful results of helping people, claiming that by contributing to the *Writer explains objections to her thesis in this paragraph.* increased survival rates of those who would otherwise have a relatively low life expectancy, wealthier people would increase the world's population and thus increase the rate at which natural resources are consumed and environmental problems arise. Although starvation is an

*An endnote would go at the end of this sentence.*

evil, Hardin says, helping the poor would create an even greater evil— increased numbers of starving people and fewer resources to help them. Others argue that just because affluent people have a relatively higher income than others, it does not follow that they are morally responsible for those who do not.

4 I believe, in contrast, that people do have a moral obligation to *Writer launches counterarguments here.* help the desperately poor. For several reasons, it is not the case that helping the poor would necessarily increase population and thus increase environmental degradation. First, while monetary aid could bring medical supplies and food and thus increase population, it could also bring contraceptive devices and increased education about population control. And so, helping the poor could actually decrease the rate of population

3

growth and, in the end, save environmental resources. Secondly, helping to reduce absolute poverty would also bring about more people who would be in a position economically, socially, and medically to contribute to cleaning up environmental problems and helping solve overpopulation problems. Finally, from a purely practical point of view, it is important to note that people are an economic resource at least as important as firewood and fertile soil, and to allow people to sicken and die is to spoil and waste that resource.

5 The obligation to help the poor is, to a certain extent, simply a matter of human rights. We believe that our pets have a right to decent treatment—enough food to live, shelter from the cold, medical care when they are hurt or ill, and affluent people in America spend large amounts of income to provide for these basic needs for animals. If animals have these rights, then surely humans have at least the same basic rights. People should be treated with more respect and consideration than animals by being given the chance to live in better surroundings than those afforded to animals.

*Here is first argument for thesis.*

6 However, the primary reason why the affluent have an obligation to help the poor has to do with the moral principle that killing another human being is wrong. If it is wrong to kill another person, then it is also morally wrong to allow someone to die, when you know they are going to die otherwise, and when it is within your means to save their lives at relatively little cost to yourself. By not acting to reduce the harmful, lethal

*Here is second argument for thesis.*

4

effects of poverty on the world's poor, affluent people are violating a

primary moral principle. Therefore, it is a moral responsibility of the rich

to help the poor.

7 In conclusion, affluent people should give a certain percentage of

their wealth to help do away with absolute poverty in the world, because

people are not only living beings who have a right to decent lives, but

because it is wrong to allow people to die when helping them live is well

within your means.

*The paper's conclusion and a restatement of the thesis.*

Paragraph 2 provides further background in the form of some **definitions of key terms**. "Relatively affluent," the writer says, means "rich or wealthy in the context of a given society." She cites philosopher Peter Singer's definition of a "fair percentage" of earnings—10 per cent. To define "absolute poverty," she quotes Robert McNamara, someone she believes has the proper credentials to offer an authoritative opinion. Absolute poverty, he says, is a condition "characterized by malnutrition, illiteracy, disease, squalid surroundings, high infant mortality and low life expectancy that is beneath any reasonable definition of human decency."

The body of the paper begins in paragraph 3, where the writer **explains the objections** to her thesis. Discussing the objections early is a good strategy when they are thought to be especially strong or foremost in the reader's mind. Dispatching them promptly prepares the way for the writer's own arguments. In many papers, however, objections are dealt with *after* the writer puts forth his or her own arguments.

In paragraph 3 the writer describes two objections in the form of arguments, one of which she considers the strongest against her position. Her approach is exactly right. Dealing with the most robust objection you can find will actually strengthen your case. On the other hand, to pick a weak objection to demolish is to lapse into the straw man fallacy, almost a guarantee that your argument will not be as strong as it could be (*Rule 3-5*). Moreover, in this situation, the strongest objection has been offered previously by a knowledgeable critic and is part of a real-world controversy.

The strongest argument against the thesis says that rich people have no moral obligation to aid the poor because helping them would actually *increase* the number of starving people in the world. Helping the poor would only multiply their numbers, raising the world's population while diminishing its population-sustaining resources. The second argument takes another approach: from the mere fact that the wealthy are relatively better off than others, it does not follow that they have a moral obligation to share their prosperity with those less fortunate.

After detailing the arguments against her thesis, in paragraph 4 the writer immediately launches a **counterargument** to show that aiding the poor would not necessarily multiply their numbers and their misery. Her three premises are: (1) although giving money to help the poor might increase their population, it might also diminish it by providing them with methods of contraception and educating them about population control; (2) reducing absolute poverty would shrink the world's population by increasing the number of people who have the wherewithal to help curb population growth and environmental harm; (3) people themselves are economic resources that can be used for the benefit of the world.

Notice that the writer does not immediately respond to the second argument against her thesis ("From the mere fact that the wealthy are relatively better off than others, it does not follow that they have a moral obligation to share their prosperity with those less fortunate.") That is, she does not try right away to show that its conclusion is false. She instead counters the argument later when she presents her case for her thesis. She shows, in effect, that contrary to the opposition's second argument, the wealthy do indeed have an obligation to share their prosperity with the poor.

After handling the main objection to her thesis, the writer articulates two arguments that support it. In paragraph 5, she holds that aid to the poor can be justified by an appeal to human rights. She argues that (1) if animals have a right to decent treatment, then surely people have at least the same right; (2) animals do have a right to decent treatment; (3) therefore, people have a right to at least the same level of treatment (and in fact have a right to even better treatment).

In paragraph 6, she puts forth another argument that she believes is even more important than the preceding one: (1) It is wrong to kill another person. (2) If it is wrong to kill another person, it is wrong to allow a person to die (if you can easily prevent the death). (3) If the wealthy fail to decrease absolute poverty (something they can easily do), they allow poor people to die. (4) Therefore, it is wrong for the wealthy to not help the poor (that is, they have a moral obligation to help).

Paragraph 7 presents the essay's conclusion, summarizing what the arguments (and counterarguments) have shown: wealthy people should help reduce absolute poverty.

An outline of the essay's arguments would look like this:

*Objection 1*

Unstated Premise • If helping the poor would actually increase the number of starving people in the world, rich people should not help the poor.

Premise • Helping the poor would actually increase the number of starving people in the world.

**Conclusion** • Therefore, rich people have no moral obligation to aid the poor.

## Objection 2

**Premise** • From the mere fact that the wealthy are relatively better off than others, it does not follow that they have a moral obligation to share their prosperity with those less fortunate.

**Conclusion** • Therefore, it does not follow that the wealthy have a moral obligation to share their prosperity with those less fortunate.

## Response to Objection 1

**Premise** • Although giving money to help the poor might increase their population, it might also diminish it by providing them with methods of contraception and educating them about population control.

**Premise** • Reducing absolute poverty would shrink the world's population by increasing the number of people who have the wherewithal to help curb population growth and environmental harm.

**Premise** • People themselves are economic resources that can be used for the benefit of the world.

**Conclusion** • Therefore, aiding the poor would not necessarily increase their numbers and their misery.

## First Argument for Thesis (and Response to Objection 2)

**Premise** • If animals have a right to decent treatment, then surely people have at least the same right.

**Premise** • Animals do have a right to decent treatment.

**Conclusion** • Therefore, people have a right to at least the same level of treatment that animals have (and in fact have a right to even better treatment).

## Second Argument for Thesis (and Response to Objection 2)

**Premise** • It is wrong to kill another person.

Premise • If it is wrong to kill another person, it is wrong to allow a person to die (if you can easily prevent the death).

Premise • If the relatively affluent fail to decrease absolute poverty (something they can easily do), they allow poor people to die.

Conclusion • Therefore, it is wrong for the relatively affluent not to decrease absolute poverty (they have a moral obligation to help the poor).

### Main Conclusion

Conclusion • Therefore, the relatively affluent have a moral obligation to decrease absolute poverty (help the poor).

In this outline you can see that the conclusions to the first and second arguments for the thesis are, essentially, the main premises for the essay's main argument, whose conclusion is "Therefore, the relatively affluent have a moral obligation to decrease absolute poverty (help the poor)."

## Writing the Essay: Step by Step

Now we examine the steps involved in crafting a good argumentative essay. You have the best chance of writing a good essay if you try to follow these steps. Just remember that the process is not linear—you may not be able to follow the steps in the sequence suggested. You may have to backtrack or rearrange the order of the steps. This kind of improvising on the fly is normal and is often necessary. At any stage in the process, you may discover that your argument is not as good as you thought, or that you did not take an important fact into account, or that you can alter the essay to make it stronger. You may then want to go back and rework your outline or tinker with the draft you are working on—and your essay will be better for it. Rethinking and revising are normal procedures for even the best writers.

Here are the steps:

1. Select a topic and narrow it to a specific issue.
2. Research the issue (where "research" can mean "think carefully about").
3. Write a thesis statement.
4. Create an outline.

5. Write a first draft.
6. Study and revise your first draft.
7. Produce a final draft.

## Step 1  Select a Topic and Narrow It to a Specific Issue

This step is first for a reason. It is here to help inexperienced writers avoid the tempting but nasty trap of picking a thesis out of the air and writing their paper on it. Caution: Any thesis that you dream up without knowing anything about it is likely to be unusable—and a waste of time. It is better to begin by selecting a topic or issue and narrowing it through research and hard thinking to a manageable thesis.

A topic is simply a broad category of subject matter, such as *human cloning, capital punishment,* or *stem cell research.* Within topics lurk an infinite number of issues—that is, questions that are in dispute. From the topic of capital punishment, for example, countless issues arise, such as whether executing criminals deters crime, whether executing a human being is ever morally permissible, whether it is ethical to execute people who are insane or mentally impaired, whether particular countries' systems of capital punishment are unfair, whether the death penalty should be mandatory for serial killers, whether executing minors is immoral, and so on. The basic idea is to select from the roster of possibilities an issue that (1) you are interested in and (2) you can adequately address in the space allowed.

Here are some issues under the topic of "God" that could be adequately addressed in a 750- to 1000-word paper (though much longer papers could also fruitfully address them):

- Is Anselm's ontological argument for the existence of God sound?
- Does William Paley's argument from design show that God exists?
- Can someone who does not believe in God behave morally?

And here are some issues whose scope is too broad to be adequately handled in a short paper:

- Does God exist?
- Are religion and science compatible?
- Does the existence of evil show that there is no God?

Often, when your instructor sets the paper assignment he or she will provide you with enough detail that you know what the issue to be addressed is. Sometimes, you may even be provided with an explicit choice of thesis statements, in that you are asked to defend a claim or its negation.

## Step 2    Research the Issue

The main reason for researching an issue is to find out what viewpoints and arguments are involved. We use the word "research" advisedly. Sometimes, the only resources you should be consulting are the course readings and your own thoughts. Careful thinking about the views related to your issue, and reasons for and against them, can result, depending on the issue, in an excellent, well-crafted paper.

If sources outside the course readings and your own head are required or seem warranted, follow up on references cited in the course readings or suggestions made by your instructor. Then make use of the library or the Internet, though be selective.

Be sure to keep careful notes of any information or ideas you encounter, including, of course, their sources, whether or not you intend to use them. You do not want, when writing your paper, to mistake someone else's words or ideas for your own, or to misattribute quotations; failing to keep track as you are researching can easily have just this sort of unfortunate result. (See Chapter 7 for more on avoiding plagiarism.)

With that in mind, let's say you begin with this issue: whether religion and contemporary morality conflict or complement each other. You probably can see right away that this issue is much too broad to be handled in a short (or long!) paper. You can restrict the scope of the issue to, for example, whether a supreme being is the foundation of moral values, a perennial question in the philosophy of religion.

Now you can explore viewpoints and arguments on all sides of the issue. You may not be able to examine *every* relevant argument, but you can probably inspect the strongest or most common ones, including some that you invent yourself. In your assessment, you want to determine what the premises are, how they relate to the conclusion, and whether they are true. (Remember, one of the best ways to test an argument is to outline it, using complete sentences, with the premises and conclusion stated as clearly as possible.) The point is to uncover a *good* argument, one worth writing and reading about. (Refer to *Rules 1-3, 1-4, 2-2, 2-3, 4-1* and *4-2*.)

The evaluation process is much the same if you decide to use more than one argument to support your thesis. The conclusion of each argument would be used in support of the thesis, just as the premises of each argument would support its conclusion. The challenge is to ensure that the connections between all the parts of the essay are clear and logical.

Suppose you narrow the God-and-morality issue to a question about the "divine command theory," the popular view that God is the foundation of morality (that an action is right if God commands it). An outline of an argument against the theory might look like this:

Premise 1 • If an action is right only because God commands it (that is, nothing is right or wrong in itself), then God's commands would be arbitrary.

Premise 2 • If an action is right only because God commands it (that is, nothing is right or wrong in itself), then abhorrent actions would be right if God commanded them.

Premise 3 • If the implications of the theory are implausible, then the theory is implausible.

Conclusion • Therefore, the theory is implausible and should be rejected.

## Step 3    Write a Thesis Statement

The conclusion of your selected argument will serve as the basis for your thesis statement. Often the conclusion *is* your thesis statement. Writing a good thesis statement is an essential step because your entire essay hinges on it.

At this stage, you should try to get the wording of your statement just right, even though you may revise it later on. Its scope should be *restricted* to what you can handle in the space you have. It should also be *focused* on just one idea, not several. Usually, it should assert, for example, that "There should not be mandatory sentencing guidelines for judges," *not* "There should not be mandatory sentencing guidelines for judges, and the system for appointing judges is flawed." This latter thesis makes two claims, not one. A good thesis statement must also be *clear*. No one should have to guess about its meaning. The thesis "The mind and the body are related to each other," for example, is insufficiently specific, since how they are allegedly related is simply absent. It gives us almost no information about what will be discussed in the essay.

It is possible to devise a thesis statement that is restricted, focused, and clear—but trivial. A trivial thesis statement is one that either concerns an insignificant issue or makes an insignificant claim. People generally don't care about insignificant issues, and few would bother to disagree with an insignificant claim. Who cares whether pens are better than pencils, or whether gambling is more fun than beachcombing? And who would care to contest the claim that pleasure is better than pain? An essay built on a trivial thesis statement wastes your readers' time (if they bother to read it at all), and you learn nothing and change nothing by writing it. Thesis statements should be *worthy*.

Here are some thesis statements that meet these criteria:

> Jeremy Bentham's moral theory known as act-utilitarianism conflicts with our common-sense ideas about human rights.

> The Canadian government should be allowed to arrest and indefinitely imprison without trial any person who is suspected of terrorism.

> Subjective relativism—the view that truth depends on what someone believes—is self-refuting.

> Racial profiling should not be used to do security screening of airline passengers.

> Canadian customs should be allowed to detain gay and lesbian publications as sexually obscene.

### Step 4    Create an Outline of the Whole Essay

If you can write out your thesis statement and outline the argument used to defend it, you have already come far. Your argument and thesis statement will constitute the skeleton of your essay. The next step is to flesh out the bones with introductory or explanatory material, responses to objections, and support for the premises (which may consist of subordinate arguments, examples, explanations, analogies, statistics, scientific research, expert opinion, or other evidence). Producing a detailed, coherent outline of the whole essay is the best way to manage this task, and if you already have an outline of your argument, creating an outline for the whole essay will be easy. An **outline** helps you fill out your argument in an orderly fashion, showing you how the pieces fit together and whether any parts are missing or misaligned. This filling-out process will probably involve checking the truth of premises, examining alternative arguments, looking for additional reasons in support, or assessing the strength of objections to your argument.

Do not be afraid to alter your outline at any stage. As you write, you may realize that your thesis is weak, your argument flawed, or your premises vague. If so, you should go back and adjust the outline before writing any further. Writing is an act of exploration, and good writers are not afraid to revise when they find something amiss.

When you outline your essay, include your full thesis statement in the introduction. Then as you work on the outline, you can refer to the statement for guidance. The major points of your outline will include the premises, conclusion, objections, and responses to objections. Here, for example, is a preliminary outline for the "divine command" essay.

I.   Introduction • (Thesis) The divine command theory is implausible and should be rejected.

   a) Explanation of theory
   b) Socrates's dilemma

II.  First Premise • If an action is right only because God commands it (that is, nothing is right or wrong in itself), then God's commands would be arbitrary—an implausible result.

   a) According to the theory, if God commands murder, then murder is right
   b) God can command anything because he is all powerful

III. Second Premise • If an action is right only because God commands it (that is, nothing is right or wrong in itself), then abhorrent actions would be right if God commanded them—another implausible result.

IV.  Objection • God would not command evil actions because he is all good.

   a) Response: The objection begs the question
   b) Response: Rachels's version of the question-begging response

V.   Third Premise • If the implications of the theory are implausible, then the theory is implausible.

VI. Conclusion • Therefore, the theory is implausible and should be rejected.

Notice that this outline indicates where objections will be addressed. Objections lodged against individual premises (and responses to them) should be shown on the outline as subpoints under the main premise divisions. Objections that are handled in one place in the body of the essay should be indicated as another major point with a Roman numeral.

Your outline should also reveal how you intend to provide support for premises that need it. This level of detail can help you head off any unpleasant surprises in the writing phase.

In many cases, the points and subpoints in your outline may correspond to the topic sentences for your essay's paragraphs. In this way, a detailed outline (in which each point is a complete sentence) can almost write your essay for you—or at least make the writing much easier.

You will find that as you tweak the outline, you may need to adjust the thesis statement. And as you perfect the thesis statement, you may need to adjust the outline. In the end, you want to satisfy yourself that the outline is complete, accurate, and structurally sound, tracing a clear and logical progression of points.

---

### Ten Common Mistakes in Argumentative Essays

1. Failing to evaluate and revise a first draft
2. Assuming that anyone's opinion is as good as anyone else's
3. Formulating a thesis that's too broad
4. Assuming that the reader can read your mind
5. Overstating what has been proven
6. Failing to start the paper early enough so that there's time for evaluation and revisions
7. Attacking an author's character instead of his or her argument
8. Presenting unsupported assertions instead of good arguments
9. Padding the essay with irrelevant or redundant passages
10. Using quotations from authors in place of well-developed arguments

The astute reader will notice that several of these mistakes are covered in more detail in other chapters.

## Step 5    Write a First Draft

Good writers revise . . . and revise and revise. They either write multiple drafts, revising in successive passes, or they revise continuously as they write. They know that their first tries will always need improvement. Inexperienced writers, on the other hand, too often dash off a first draft without a second look—then turn it in! A much more reasonable approach (and the best one for most students) is to write at least a first draft and a final draft or—better—several drafts and a final one.

Because argumentative essays require such care with articulating the argument, and because it is so difficult to write good later drafts based on a very poor initial one, the first draft should be in reasonable shape. (If it helps, don't call your first version a "draft"!)

Provide a good introduction that lays out your thesis statement, gives background information on the issue, and draws your readers into the essay. Make it interesting, informative, and pertinent to the question at hand. Do not assume that your readers will automatically see that your paper is worth reading.

Wordy and superficial introductions are a common problem with student papers. They go on and on about the topic but say little that is germane or necessary. Such intros read as if they are either just filling up space or slowly warming up to the subject. They can often be deleted entirely without any loss to the essay because the true introduction begins on page 3. The best introductions are concise, relevant—and, usually, short.

In a less formal essay, you can grab the attention of your readers and lead them into the paper by starting off with a bold statement of your thesis, a provocative scenario that encapsulates or symbolizes the issue, or a compelling fact suggesting the importance of your thesis.

In a more formal paper, the usual course is to assert your thesis statement, spell out the issue, and explain how you plan to develop your argument or how the rest of the essay will unfold (without going into lengthy detail). In short papers, you may be able to mention every premise; in long or complex essays, just stating the most important points should suffice.

Look at this introduction to the "divine command" essay (presented in its entirety later in this chapter):

[1]    Many people believe that God is a lawgiver who alone defines what actions are right and wrong. God, in other words, is the author of morality; an action is right if and only if God commands it to be done. According to this view, there is no right or wrong until God says so,

and nothing is moral or immoral independently of God's willing it to be thus. God, and only God, makes rightness and wrongness. This view is known as the divine command theory of morality.

[2]    A simple version of the theory is widely accepted today, among both the religious and non-religious. In this version, God is thought to be the source of all moral principles and values. He can be the source of all morality because he is omnipotent, being able to do anything whatsoever, including create the very foundations of right and wrong.

[3]    In the *Euthyphro*, Socrates brings out what is probably the oldest and strongest criticism of the theory. He asks, in effect, is an action right because God commands it to be done, or does God command it to be done because it is right? This question lays bare the dilemma that is inherent in the theory: if an action is right because God commands it, then there is nothing in the action itself that makes it right, and God's command is arbitrary. If God commands the action because it is right (that is, he does not make it right), then rightness would seem to be independent of (or prior to) God, and the divine command theory is false. I contend that, at least in the simplest version of the theory, this ancient dilemma still stands and that the most plausible way to resolve it is to reject the theory by accepting that moral standards must exist independently of God's commands.

This introduction is long because the issue requires considerable explanation and background. The key question of the essay, however, is raised almost immediately in the first paragraph: Does God make rightness? In paragraphs 2 and 3, the writer explains the divine command theory so that its controversial status is evident and its relevance to current views on morality is clear. After all, a version of the theory is "widely accepted today," and the question of its truth was raised by none other than Socrates. The thesis statement appears in the last sentence of paragraph 3: "Moral standards must exist independently of God's commands."

The body of your essay should state, explain, and develop your argument in full. You should present each premise, elaborate on it as necessary, and provide support for those points likely to be questioned by readers. Plan on devoting at least one paragraph to each premise, although many more may be needed to make your case.

Every paragraph in your paper should relate to the thesis; every sentence in each paragraph should relate to a topic sentence. Delete any sentence that does not serve the essay's purpose. Ensure that paragraphs appear in a logical sequence and are clearly linked by transitional words and phrases or references to material in preceding paragraphs. Your readers should never have to wonder what the connection is between parts of your paper.

In our example essay, these two paragraphs follow the introduction:

[4]  The central argument against the notion that rightness is whatever God commands is this: if an action is right only because God commands it (that is, nothing is right or wrong in itself, or independent of God), then cruelty, murder, torture, and many other terrible actions would be right if God commanded them. If God commanded such acts, then they would be right, and no one would be committing a wrong by doing them. On the simple version of the theory, there are no limits whatsoever to God's power, so he could indeed command such things. If nothing would be right or wrong until God wills it, he could have no reason to either command murder or forbid it, to sanction the torture of innocents or prohibit it. Therefore, if God commands rightness, God's commands would be arbitrary—a result that would be implausible to the religious and non-religious alike.

[5]  A parallel argument is also possible. As stated above, if an action is right only because God commands it, then cruelty, murder, torture, and many other terrible actions would be right if God commanded them. This means that such immoral actions—immoral in light of common moral standards—could be transformed by God into moral actions. This outcome, however, would also be implausible to both the religious and non-religious.

This essay presents two separate arguments to support its thesis statement—one in paragraph 4 and one in paragraph 5. Paragraph 4 argues that if God commands (makes) rightness, then his commands are arbitrary, a point expressed in the topic sentence (the last one in the paragraph). Paragraph 5 argues that if God commands rightness, he could make immoral actions moral, and this too is implausible. This argument also appears in the paragraph's topic sentence (the sentence beginning "This means that . . .").

In most cases, your essay will need a conclusion. It may simply reiterate the thesis statement (ideally without repeating it word for word). In long, formal, or complex papers, the conclusion may include a summary of the essay's arguments. In short or simple essays, there may be no need for a conclusion; the point of the whole essay may be evident and emphatic without a conclusion. If you are unsure whether your paper needs a conclusion, take no chances—include one.

The conclusion, however, is not the place to launch into a completely different issue, make entirely unsubstantiated claims, malign those who disagree with you, or pretend that your argument is stronger than it really is. These tactics will not strengthen your essay but weaken it.

## Step 6    Study and Revise Your First Draft

Your first draft is likely to have problems both big and small. At this stage, however, you should scrutinize mostly the big ones. This is no time for proofreading (correcting spelling, fixing punctuation, repairing typos, and the like). This is the time to make substantive changes such as those listed here. Put your paper aside for a while, then read it critically and do the following:

- *Examine your argument first.* Check to see that the premises are properly related to the conclusion and that they are adequately supported. Does the conclusion follow from the premises? Are the premises true? Is the supporting evidence solid? Would a reader be convinced by this argument? Rewrite the argument, or parts of it, if need be.

- *Check for unity.* Make sure that every paragraph relates to the thesis statement and discusses just one idea. Delete or modify paragraphs and sentences that go off on tangents. Remove any padding, passages that are irrelevant to the essay but are inserted to lengthen the paper or make it seem more impressive.

- *Test for clarity.* As you read the paper, ask yourself whether the thesis is stated clearly. Does the paper's introduction tell the reader what the essay is about and how the argument will unfold? Do the topic sentences need to be more explicit? Are there points that need to be emphasized more? Are ideas and premises adequately explained? Are the connections among ideas clear? Are there appropriate transitions to keep readers on track? Revise for maximum clarity.

- *Hunt for repetitions.* Look for phrasing in which you have repeated ideas or words unnecessarily. Are you just repeating yourself rather than fully developing your points? Cut out or rewrite suspect passages.

- *Think your paper through.* Ask yourself if you are really *engaged* in the critical thinking required to produce a good paper. Are you just repeating what your sources say without fully understanding them? Are you assuming, without checking, that certain statements are true? Are you ignoring contrary evidence or contradictions? Are you going for the obvious and the simplistic when you should be trying to address complexity?
- *Smooth out the language.* Fix awkward sentences, grammatical errors, wordy constructions, pretentious phrasing, and other impediments to clear communication. (See Chapters 8 and 9.)
- *Show your draft to others.* Even if those who read your paper know little about philosophy, they should be able to understand your thesis statement, your argument, and all important points. They should be able to tell from the introduction exactly what you are trying to do in your paper. If any part of the essay is confusing to them, consider rewriting that passage.

After writing and revising your first draft, repeat the process, creating as many drafts as necessary. Your goal is to revise until you have made all the necessary substantive changes.

### Step 7    Produce a Final Draft

After completing all substantive changes, you should generate a final draft, the one you will turn in. The final draft should reflect not only the big changes, but also the corrections of all minor errors as well—misspellings, typos, grammatical errors, misplaced words, faulty punctuation, and documentation mistakes. This task should be primarily a proofreading job. At this stage, you should also format the manuscript according to your instructor's requirements. (If no requirements are specified, follow the guidelines given in Appendix A.)

The key to producing a clean final draft is downtime—an interim in which you leave the last draft alone and focus on something else. Coming back to your paper after a day or so away from it can help you see errors that passed right by you before. You may be surprised how many mistakes this fresh look can reveal, especially if you read the paper out loud. You could, if this is permitted by your instructor, ask a friend to read your paper and give you some constructive criticism. Be sure, though, that *you* are the author of any changes you make.

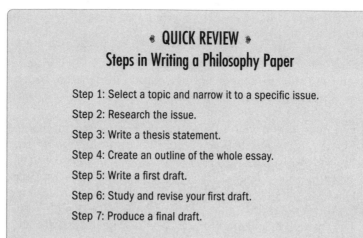

**⟡ QUICK REVIEW ⟡**

**Steps in Writing a Philosophy Paper**

Step 1: Select a topic and narrow it to a specific issue.

Step 2: Research the issue.

Step 3: Write a thesis statement.

Step 4: Create an outline of the whole essay.

Step 5: Write a first draft.

Step 6: Study and revise your first draft.

Step 7: Produce a final draft.

## An Annotated Sample Paper

The following is the full version of the divine command essay, which demonstrates many of the considerations discussed in this chapter—organization, argument, thesis, explanation, sentence clarity, and more.

## The Divine Command Theory

1 Many people believe that God is a lawgiver who alone defines what actions are right and wrong. God, in other words, is the author of morality; an action is right if and only if God commands it to be done. According to this view, there is no right or wrong until God says so, and nothing is moral or immoral independently of God's willing it to be thus. God, and only God, *makes* rightness and wrongness. This view is known as the divine command theory of morality.

*Introduces topic.*

*Defines key term.*

2 A simple version of the theory is widely accepted today, among both the religious and nonreligious. In this version, God is thought to be the source of all moral principles and values. He can be the source of all morality because he is omnipotent, being able to do anything whatsoever, including create the very foundations of right and wrong.

*Specifies the version of the theory to be discussed.*

*Source is cited.*

3 In the *Euthyphro*, Socrates brings out what is probably the oldest and strongest criticism of the theory. He asks, in effect, is an action right because God commands it to be done, or does God command it to be done because it is right?[1] This question lays bare the dilemma that is inherent in the theory: If an action is right because God commands it, then there is nothing in the action itself that makes it right, and God's command is arbitrary. If God commands the action because it is right (that is, he does not *make* it right), then rightness would seem to be independent of (or prior to) God, and the divine command theory is false. I contend that, at

*Provides further background on issue.*

2

least in the simplest version of the theory, this ancient dilemma still stands and that the most plausible way to resolve it is to reject the theory by accepting that moral standards must exist independently of God's commands.

*Thesis statement.*

4 The central argument against the notion that rightness is whatever God commands is this: If an action is right only because God commands it (that is, nothing is right or wrong in itself, or independent of God), then cruelty, murder, torture, and many other terrible actions would be right if God commanded them. If God commanded such acts, then they would be right, and no one would be committing a wrong by doing them. On the simple version of the theory, there are no limits whatsoever to God's power, so he could indeed command such things. If nothing would be right or wrong until God wills it, he could have no reason to either command murder or forbid it, to sanction the torture of innocents or prohibit it. Therefore, if God commands rightness, God's commands would be arbitrary—a result that would be implausible to the religious and nonreligious alike.

*Writer presents first argument for thesis.*

5 A parallel argument is also possible. As stated above, if an action is right only because God commands it, then cruelty, murder, torture, and many other terrible actions would be right if God commanded them. This means that such immoral actions—immoral in light of common moral standards—could be transformed by God into moral actions. This

*Writer presents second argument for thesis.*

3

outcome, however, would also be implausible to both the religious and

nonreligious.

6 The main objection to the above arguments is that God would

never command us to commit heinous acts. He would not because he is

morally perfect—all-good in all ways. This counterargument, however,

begs the question; it is a circular argument. The divine command theory is

offered to explain what makes an action right—what makes something

morally good. But to try to define what good is by saying that God is good

is to talk in a circle: God's commands are good, and they are good because

they are God's commands. This definition reduces the divine command

theory to empty doubletalk. If we wish to have a better understanding of

what makes an action right, we cannot be satisfied with such a definition.

*Writer explains and rebuts main objection to thesis.*

7 Moral philosopher James Rachels makes this same argument in a

slightly different way.

*Quotation is introduced.*

8 [If] we accept the idea that good and bad are defined by

reference to God's will, this notion is deprived of any meaning.

What could it mean to say that God's commands are good? If "X is

good" means "X is commanded by God," then "God's commands

are good" would mean only "God's commands are commanded by

God," an empty truism.[2]

*Quote from source, with endnote.*

4

9 To return to Socrates' dilemma, either an action is right only because God commands it, or an action is right (or wrong) independently of God's commands. As we have seen, if an action is right only because God commands it, then God's commands must be arbitrary, and it is possible for him to sanction obviously immoral acts. Since both these consequences are unacceptable, we must accept the second alternative: Rightness must be independent of (or prior to) God's commands. We therefore must reject the simplest version of the divine command theory.

*Conclusion.*

*Summary of arguments for thesis and thesis restatement.*

---

[1]Plato, *Euthyphro* in *The Trial and Death of Socrates* (Cambridge: Hackett, 1975).
[2]James Rachels, *The Elements of Moral Philosophy* (New York: McGraw-Hill Higher Education, 2003), 51.

*For discussion:*

- What kinds of papers, aside from exegetical and argumentative essays, are there?
- How different are expository and argumentative essays?
- Some people promote the "Five-Paragraph Essay" (an essay consisting of one introductory paragraph, three body paragraphs, and a concluding paragraph). Is this a good model for writing an essay? Why or why not?

*For further information:*

- See www.sfu.ca/~horban/writing1.htm for excellent help in writing a philosophy paper. The advice is aimed at writers new to philosophy, but would be helpful even to seasoned writers.[2]
- As always, consult your instructor.

# Notes

1. Kathleen Dean Moore, "Should Relatively Affluent People Help the Poor?" This paper follows an outline written by her student, Brian Figur. Reproduced by permission of the author.
2. Peter Horban, "Writing a Philosophy Paper," © 1993, referenced with permission.

# ❧ 6 ❧

# Avoiding Fallacious Reasoning

As you surely must realize by now, arguments are the main focus of most philosophical writing. Recall that an argument is a combination of statements in which *some* are intended to combine in support of *one*. The statement meant to be supported is the conclusion; the statements meant to do the supporting are the premises. The premises are supposed to be the reasons for accepting the conclusion. As a reader of philosophy, you want to determine whether the arguments you encounter are good ones. As a writer of philosophy, you want to ensure that the arguments you use to make your case are also good. You want to avoid being fooled by, or fooling others with, a bad argument.

You can become more proficient in these skills if you know how to identify fallacies when you see them. **Fallacies** are common but bad arguments. They are defective arguments that appear so often in writing and speech that philosophers have given them names and offered instructions on how to recognize and avoid them. Many fallacies are not just failed arguments—they are also deceptively plausible appeals, apt to mislead you or your readers.

This chapter reviews many of the most common fallacies (some having been introduced in Chapter 3) and explains why they are bogus so that you can detect them in your everyday reading and writing.

## Straw Man

The **straw man fallacy** is the misrepresentation of a person's views so he or she can be more easily attacked or dismissed. (See Chapter 3 for more discussion.) Let's say you're arguing that a particular war in which Canada is involved is too costly in lives and money, and your opponent replies this way:

My adversary argues that this war is much too difficult for Canada
and that we ought to, in effect, cut and run while we can. But why
must we take the coward's way out?

Your point has been distorted, made to look more extreme or radi-
cal than it really is; it is now an easy target. The notion that we ought
to "cut and run" or "take the coward's way out" *does not follow* from
the statement that the particular war is too costly.

The straw man distortion, of course, proves nothing, although many
people fall for it every day. This fallacy is probably the most common
type of fallacious reasoning used in politics. It is also popular in many
other kinds of argumentation—including student philosophy papers.

## Ad Hominem

Closely related to the straw man fallacy is the **ad hominem fallacy**
(also known as the **appeal to the person fallacy**). Ad hominem rejects
a statement on the grounds that it comes from a particular person,
not because the statement itself is false or dubious. Here's an example:

Wong argues that our current welfare system is defective. But don't
listen to her—she's a libertarian.

This argument is defective because it asks us to reject a claim
because of a person's character, background, or circumstances—things
that are generally irrelevant to the truth of claims. A statement must
stand or fall *on its own merits*. The personal characteristics of the person espousing the view do not necessarily have a bearing on its truth
(see Chapter 3). Only if we can show that someone's traits somehow
make the claim dubious are we justified in rejecting the claim because
of a person's personal characteristics, but such a circumstance is rare.

A variant on this fallacy is arguing that a claim is true on the
grounds that a person the arguer likes or admires has made it. Unless
there is reason to think that this person is a good source of information about the subject at hand, his or her "testimony" is not relevant.
For example, if you learned that your favourite movie star (whose political views and experience are unknown to you) claims that a certain
politician should be the next prime minister, you should not weigh this
when deciding how to vote. (In contrast, if your doctor were to recommend getting a flu shot, claiming that it will preserve your good health,
you should certainly treat this as relevant in deciding what to do.)

## ❦ Ad Hominem Attacks in Your Paper ❧

Ad hominem arguments often creep into student philosophy papers. Part of the reason is that some appeals to the person are not so obvious. For example:

- "Swinburne's cosmological argument is a serious attempt to show that God is the best explanation for the existence of the universe. However, he is a well-known theist, and this fact raises some doubts about the strength of his case."

- "Dennett argues from the materialist standpoint, so he begins with a bias that we need to take into account."

- "Some of the strongest arguments against the death penalty come from a few people who are actually on death row. They obviously have a vested interest in showing that capital punishment is morally wrong. We therefore are forced to take their arguments—however convincing—with a grain of salt."

# Appeal to Popularity

**Appeal to popularity** (or **appeal to the masses**) is another extremely common fallacy. It argues that a claim must be true not for good reasons but simply because many people believe it. The idea is that, somehow, there is truth in numbers. For example:

> Of course there is life after death. Everyone believes that.

> Seventy per cent of Canadians believe that the government's tax cuts are good for the economy. So don't try to tell me the tax cuts aren't good for the economy.

> Most people believe that Jones is guilty, so she's guilty.

In each of these arguments, the conclusion is thought to be true merely because an impressive number of people believe it. The number of people who believe a claim, however, is irrelevant to the claim's truth. Large groups of people have been—and are—wrong about many things. Many people once believed that the Earth is flat, mermaids are real, and human sacrifices help crops grow. They were wrong.

## Appeal to Tradition

**Appeal to tradition** is actually a kind of appeal to popularity. It is arguing that merely because a claim is sanctioned by tradition, it must be true. This says, in effect, that a statement is true because it has been held (or approved of) for a long time. Appeal to tradition is fallacious because the longevity of a traditional claim is logically irrelevant to its truth. Claims backed by a long tradition can be wrong—and often are. Consider the following:

> Youths who commit heinous crimes should be tried as adults. This view has been the traditional stand that this community has always taken. There can be no doubt about it.

> Ancient shaman medicine works. First Nations people have used it for thousands of years.

On the other hand, dismissing a claim just because it is traditional is also fallacious. The mere fact that a claim is traditional is no good reason for rejecting it. Rejection or acceptance must be based on adequate grounds.

## Genetic Fallacy

Similar to the ad hominem fallacy, the **genetic fallacy** argues that a statement can be judged true or false based on its source. In the ad hominem fallacy, someone's character or situation is erroneously thought to be relevant; in the genetic fallacy, the truth of a statement supposedly depends on origins other than an individual—organizations, political platforms, groups, schools of thought, even exceptional states of mind (like dreams and intuitions). Look at the following examples:

> That new military reform idea must be bunk. It comes from a socialist think tank.

> At the city council meeting, Hernando said that he had a plan to curb the number of car accidents on Highway 19. But you can bet that whatever it is, it's a silly plan—he said it came to him when he was stoned.

The senate is considering a proposal to reform employment equity, but you know their ideas must be ridiculous. What do they know about the rights of the disadvantaged? They're a bunch of rich white guys.

As in the ad hominem fallacy, the genetic fallacy fails to engage with the content of the claim or any argument for it.

## Equivocation

The fallacy of **equivocation** assigns two different meanings to the same significant word in an argument. The word is used in one sense in a premise and in a different sense in another place in the argument. The switch in meaning can deceive the reader and disrupt the argument, rendering it invalid or weaker than it would be otherwise. Here's a classic example:

> Only man is rational.
> No woman is a man.
> Therefore, no woman is rational.

And one other:

> You are a bad writer.
> If you are a bad writer, then you are a bad person.
> Therefore, you are a bad person.

The first argument equivocates on the word *man*. In the first premise, *man* means *humankind*; in the second, *male*. Thus, the argument seems to prove that women are not rational. You can see the trick better if you assign the same meaning to both instances of *man*, like this:

> Only humans are rational.
> No woman is a human.
> Therefore, no woman is rational.

In the second argument, the equivocal term is *bad*. In the first premise, *bad* means incompetent; in the second, immoral.

## Appeal to Ignorance

As its name implies, this fallacy tries to prove something by appealing to what we *don't* know. **Appeal to ignorance** is arguing either that (1) a claim is true because it hasn't been proven false, or (2) a claim is false because it hasn't been proven true. For example:

> Try as they may, scientists have never been able to disprove the existence of an afterlife. The conclusion to be drawn from this is that there is in fact an afterlife.

> Super Green Algae can cure cancer. No scientific study has ever shown that it does not work.

> No one has ever shown that ESP (extrasensory perception) is real. Therefore, it does not exist.

> There is no evidence that people on welfare are hard-working and responsible. Therefore, they are not hard-working and responsible.

The first two arguments try to prove a claim by pointing out that it hasn't been proven false. The second two try to prove that a claim is false because it hasn't been proven true. Both kinds of arguments are bogus because they assume that a lack of evidence proves something. A lack of evidence, however, can prove nothing. Being ignorant of the facts does not enlighten us.

Notice that if a lack of evidence could prove something, then you could prove just about anything you wanted. You could reason, for instance, that since no one can prove that you do *not* possess supernatural powers, you *do* possess them.

Appeal to ignorance often takes the form of asking someone to prove a *universal negative*. A universal negative is a claim that nothing of a particular kind exists. Can you prove that flying horses don't exist? How about unicorns or centaurs? Such requests for proof are utterly unreasonable because they ask the impossible. To prove that flying horses or unicorns don't exist, you would have to do something that no one can do—search all space and time. You can, of course, prove a more limited negative claim, such as "There are no books in this house" or "There are no fish in this pond." Requests for proof of a universal negative, however, are both absurd and unfair.

## False Dilemma

In a dilemma, you are forced to choose between two unattractive possibilities. The fallacy of **false dilemma** is arguing erroneously that since there are only two alternatives to choose from, and one of them is unacceptable, the other one must be true. Consider these examples:

> You have to listen to reason. Either you must sell your car to pay your rent, or your landlord will throw you out on the street. You obviously aren't going to sell your car, so you will be evicted.

> You have to face the hard facts about the war on drugs. Either we must spend billions of dollars to increase military and law enforcement operations against drug cartels, or we must legalize all drugs. We obviously are not going to legalize all drugs, so we have to spend billions on anti-cartel operations.

The first argument limits you to only two choices: either sell your car or get evicted. This argument is fallacious if the first premise is false—that is, if more alternatives exist. In this case, presumably, you could get a job, borrow money from a friend, or sell your DVD player and TV. If the argument seems convincing, it is because these other possibilities are ignored.

The second argument asserts that we have only two ways to go: spend billions to attack drug cartels or legalize all drugs. This "either/or" premise, however, is false; there are at least three other options: the billions could be spent to prevent drug use and to reduce harm, drug producers could be given monetary incentives to switch to non-drug businesses, or only some drugs could be legalized.

## Begging the Question

The fallacy of **begging the question** is trying to prove a conclusion by using that very same conclusion as support. Begging the question is arguing in a circle. This way of trying to demonstrate a claim is, in effect, "x is true because x is true." This is, of course, valid! But it should not be persuasive for anybody who does not already accept the conclusion. Few people would fall for this fallacy in such a simple form, but more subtle kinds can be beguiling. For example, here's a classic instance of begging the question:

The Bible says that God exists.
The Bible is true because God wrote it.
Therefore, God exists.

The conclusion here ("God exists") rests on premises that assume that very conclusion.

Here's another one:

All citizens have the right to a fair trial because those whom the state is obliged to protect and give consideration are automatically due judicial criminal proceedings that are equitable by any reasonable standard.

This passage may at first seem like a good argument, but it isn't. It reduces to this unimpressive assertion: "All citizens have the right to a fair trial because all citizens have the right to a fair trial." The conclusion is "All citizens have the right to a fair trial," but that's more or less what the premise says. The premise—"those whom the state is obliged to protect and give consideration are automatically due judicial criminal proceedings that are equitable by any reasonable standard"—is equivalent to "All citizens have the right to a fair trial."

When circular reasoning is subtle, it can ensnare even its own creators. The fallacy can easily sneak into an argument if the premise and conclusion say the same thing but in different, complicated ways.

## Hasty Generalization

The fallacy of **hasty generalization** is drawing a conclusion about a whole group or class of things based on an inadequate sample of the group. For example:

All three of the university professors I've met in my lifetime were bald. Therefore, all university professors are bald.

I interviewed 100 students at Laval University, and 40 of them were Liberals. Therefore, 40 per cent of all university students in Canada are Liberals.

For a whole week, I stood outside the art museum and interviewed people entering or leaving the building. I asked them if they listened to CBC Radio, and 70 per cent said that they did. Obviously, most of the people in this city listen to CBC Radio.

A sample can be inadequate because it is too small or not representative enough. In the first argument, the sample is ridiculously inadequate. The most obvious problem, of course, is that it's much too small. (It is also unrepresentative.) You can draw no reliable conclusions about all university professors based on a sample of three.

The sample in the second argument is also inadequate. No matter how large the sample is at Laval, it will not be representative of all university students. It is unreasonable not to be concerned about regional variations. There is no good reason to think that the political views of students at Laval are representative of students from all Canadian universities. (Without knowing more, drawing a conclusion about even Laval students is problematic.)

The sample in the third argument suffers from the same problem. Since the survey was conducted in front of an art museum, the sample is likely to reflect the preferences of museum patrons, not of the whole city. The sample, whether large or small, will not be representative enough.

## Slippery Slope

The metaphor behind this fallacy suggests the danger of stepping on a precarious incline, losing your footing, and sliding to disaster. The fallacy of **slippery slope**, then, is arguing erroneously that a particular action should not be taken because it will lead inevitably to other actions resulting in some dire outcome. The key word here is *erroneously*. A slippery slope scenario becomes fallacious when there is no reason to believe that the chain of events predicted will ever happen. For example:

> We must reverse the decision to allow gay marriage. Allowing it debases and devalues traditional marriage between a man and a woman, which will lead to an increase in divorces. And higher divorce rates can only harm our children.

This argument is fallacious because there are no reasons for believing that gay marriage will ultimately result in the chain of events described. If good reasons could be given, the argument might be salvaged.

## Appeal to Pity and Appeal to Fear

Both of these fallacies, **appeal to pity** and **appeal to fear**, were discussed in Chapter 3 (see *Rule 3-8*). That one feels pity for a person who could be convicted of a crime is not a reason to think that the person did not commit the crime. Similarly, that one is afraid of the consequences of a proposition being true or being believed to be true is no reason to think the proposition is false.

> I'll be really sad if you fail the course. Therefore, you should not fail the course.

> If people believe that the banking system is faulty, they will lose faith in it and anarchy will ensue. Therefore, the banking system is not faulty.

## Fallacy of Composition

Sometimes what is true about the parts of a thing is also true of the whole—and sometimes not. The **fallacy of composition** argues erroneously that what can be said of the parts can also be said of the whole. Consider the following:

> Each piece of wood that makes up this house is lightweight. Therefore, the whole house is lightweight.

> The monthly payments on this car are low. Hence, the cost of the car is low.

Television advertisements often use an argument like that last one, but you don't need to be a math genius to see that the total cost of a car might be very high, even with low monthly payments. Likewise, a very heavy object can be made with parts that, individually, weigh very little, and we have all seen teams fail to perform well despite the high skill level of individual team members. However, sometimes the whole does have the same properties as the parts. If each part of the rocket is made of steel, the whole rocket is made of steel.

# Fallacy of Division

If you turn the fallacy of composition upside down, you get the **fallacy of division**—arguing erroneously that what can be said of the whole can be said of the parts:

The house is heavy. Therefore, every part of the house is heavy.

The platoon is very effective. Therefore, every member of the platoon is effective.

That herd of elephants eats an enormous amount of food each day. Therefore, each elephant in the herd eats an enormous amount of food each day.

---

## ❀ QUICK REVIEW ❀
## Common Fallacies

- **Straw Man**
  The misrepresentation of a person's views so he or she can be more easily attacked or dismissed. (See *Rule 3-6*.)

- **Ad Hominem (Appeal to the Person)**
  Rejecting a statement on the grounds that it comes from a particular person, not because the statement or claim itself is false or dubious. (See *Rule 3-6*.)

- **Appeal to Popularity**
  Arguing that a claim must be true not because it is backed by good reasons but simply because many people believe it.

- **Appeal to Tradition**
  Arguing that merely because a claim is sanctioned by tradition, it must be true.

- **Genetic Fallacy**
  Arguing that a statement can be judged true or false based on its source.

- **Equivocation**
  Assigning two different meanings to the same word in an argument. (See *Rule 3-7* for a discussion of ambiguity.)

- **Appeal to Ignorance**
  Arguing either that (1) a claim is true because it hasn't been proven false, or (2) a claim is false because it hasn't been proven true.

- **False Dilemma**
  Arguing erroneously that since there are only two alternatives to choose from, and one of them is unacceptable, the other one must be true.

- **Begging the Question**
  Trying to prove a conclusion by using that very conclusion as a premise.

- **Hasty Generalization**
  Drawing a conclusion about a whole group or class of things based on an inadequate sample of the group.

- **Slippery Slope**
  Arguing erroneously that a particular action should not be taken because it will lead inevitably to other actions resulting in some dire outcome.

- **Appeal to Pity**
  Arguing that a claim is true on the grounds that if it is not accepted as true, someone will suffer, or that it should be accepted as true because someone has suffered. (See *Rule 3-8*.)

- **Appeal to Fear**
  Arguing that a claim is true on the grounds that if it is not accepted as true, something really bad will happen. (See *Rule 3-8* and slippery slope above.)

- **Fallacy of Composition**
  Arguing erroneously that what can be said of the parts can be said of the whole.

- **Fallacy of Division**
  Arguing erroneously that what can be said of the whole can be said of the parts.

*For discussion:*

- Make up your own examples of each kind of fallacy.

- Are there some arguments that resemble these fallacies but that are not, in fact, fallacious? If you think there are, try to produce some examples. If you think there are not, try to produce some seeming examples and explain why they are still fallacious.

# ❧ 7 ❧
# Using, Quoting, and Citing Sources

Probably very few writers compose philosophy papers without relying at some point and in some way on other writings—essays, books, journals, magazines, and reference works. Reliance on such sources generally makes for better philosophy papers. (Be aware, though, of the common tendency to canvass too many sources instead of thinking hard about the assigned readings and the topic given. In many classes, the best papers do *not* use sources outside those discussed in class.) Many writers do not know how to use sources (class material or not) properly and productively, and their papers (and grades) suffer. The following discussion should serve as a useful reference whenever you are using sources.

But before we get to this, a word is in order about the use of the Internet. Be aware that your instructor has the discretion to forbid the use of Internet (or even any outside) sources. Make sure you know what is permissible before you begin work on your paper. If Internet sources are forbidden, resist the temptation to do an Internet search! If you do a search and find something interesting, you will not be able to use it as you will not be allowed to cite it. (Using it without citing would constitute plagiarism—see below.) If, however, you are allowed to cite Internet sources, you must be a careful consumer and record keeper. Not all Internet sources are reliable; contrary to what you may believe, sources such as Wikipedia are not infallible! Almost anybody can post a webpage that looks professional. Though it will be difficult at first when you don't know a lot about your topic, try to be discerning, and don't trust search engines to show you the best sites. Remember that you will often find reputable sources affiliated with institutes of higher education.

Citing your sources properly is as important as choosing them properly. You should keep scrupulous notes about any sites you visit, whether or not you think you will be referring to them in your paper. If you don't record your research and you do need that information later on, tracking it down could prove difficult and time-consuming. See Appendix B for some conventions on citing web sources.

### Rule 7-1    Know When and How to Quote Sources

To quote something is to use someone's exact words in your own writing. You should decide to quote only for good reasons. One such reason is that the author's words are the clearest or best expression of a point you want to make (otherwise a paraphrase or summary may be more effective). Another reason is that you are criticizing or explaining the author's claim or argument and it is important to show precisely how the author expresses it. In general, you should not use quotations for reasons *unrelated* to your paper's thesis. For example, you should not quote just because you cannot think of anything to say, because you want to disguise your lack of understanding of the material, or because you want to stretch your paper to the required length. Your instructor will see through these tactics.

Quotations are not like seasoning; they cannot be sprinkled randomly throughout your paper to improve its overall flavour. Every quotation must be properly introduced and explained. (See Chapter 4 for discussion.) When you quote material, you must ensure that your reader knows who wrote it and how it is related to your thesis as well as the point at hand. Your reader should never have to think, "Whose words are these, and what do they have to do with this discussion?"

Here are some examples of common ways to incorporate quotations into your paper:

> Even if there is an evil genius, Descartes believes that there is at least one thing that he knows, namely, that he exists. "Then without doubt I exist also if he deceives me," Descartes says, "and let him deceive me as much as he will, he can never cause me to be nothing so long as I think that I am something."[1]

> This argument starts from a fact about the world and then tries to show that the existence of God is the best explanation of that fact. Richard Gale, however, points out that the most serious objection

that can be raised against the God of the cosmological argument is that "it is impossible for such a being to exist, thereby showing that this argument's conclusion is necessarily false."[2]

Notice that to signal the beginning and ending of the words of a quotation, you insert quotation marks before and after them. Except in a few cases noted later in this chapter, none other than the author's precise wording is allowed between the quotation marks—no paraphrase, no summary, no added words.

Very long quotations are set off without quotation marks in what is known as block form. Customarily, quotations of four to ten manuscript lines are put in block form. Block quotes are usually separated from regular text by leaving extra space above and below the block quote and by indenting its left edge. For example:

> If a prediction turns out to be false, we can always save the hypothesis by modifying the background theory. As Philip Kitcher notes:
>
>> Individual scientific claims do not, and cannot, confront the evidence one by one. Rather . . . we can only test relatively large bundles of claims. What this means is that when our experiments go awry we are not logically compelled to select any particular claim as the culprit. We can always save a cherished hypothesis from refutation by rejecting (however implausibly) one of the other members of the bundle.[3]

As mentioned earlier, direct quotations should match the original passage word for word. The corollary to this rule is that you may alter quotations (1) if the change does not distort the author's meaning and (2) if the change is properly signalled to the reader. Writers sometimes alter quotations to make them easier to read or to eliminate extraneous material, as in the example just given.

One way to indicate that a quotation has been altered is to use ellipsis marks—three consecutive dots, or periods, with a space before and after each one. You use ellipsis marks to show that words have been omitted from a quotation. Use them to indicate an omission inside a sentence.

> William Frankena argues that any adequate moral theory must incorporate some principle of justice but that the principle must not

be too broad. As he points out, "Treating people equally . . . does not mean making their lives equally good or maintaining their lives at the same level of goodness."⁴

Here, the words "in this sense" have been omitted; they are unnecessary because the intended sense has already been established.

Also use ellipsis marks to show that a whole sentence or more has been omitted. If the omitted material comes after a complete sentence, insert the ellipsis dots after that sentence's period.

> Utilitarianism does not require that only the guilty be punished or that the punishment fit the crime. The categorical imperative, however, requires both. As Kant says:
>
> > But what is the mode and measure of punishment which public justice takes as its principle and standard? It is just the principle of equality, by which the pointer of the scale of justice is made to incline more to the one side than to the other. . . . Hence it may be said: "If you slander another, you slander yourself; if you steal from another, you steal from yourself; if you strike another, you strike yourself; if you kill another, you kill yourself." This is the only principle which . . . can definitely assign both the quality and the quantity of a just penalty.⁵

Another way to signal that a quotation has been changed is to use square brackets like this: [ ]. Regular brackets (parentheses) might well have been in the original, so cannot serve this purpose. Use square brackets to add or substitute your own words (or sometimes even letters, when, say, a change from upper to lower case, or vice versa, is warranted) into a quotation to clarify wording or to make the quotation's grammar fit into the surrounding text.

> By questioning the control exercised by autonomous man and demonstrating the control of the environment, a science of behavior also seems to question [human] dignity and worth. [The traditional view is that a] person is responsible for his behavior, not only in the sense that he may be justly punished when he behaves badly, but also in the sense that he is to be given credit and admired for his achievements. A scientific analysis shifts the credit as well as the blame to the environment, and traditional practices can then no longer be justified.⁶

Remember, whether you use ellipsis marks or brackets, you must be sure *not* to misrepresent the author. (See Chapter 4.)

## Rule 7-2    Do Not Plagiarize

**Plagiarism** is theft of someone else's ideas or words, whether deliberate or accidental. (Most is accidental.) Plagiarism is a serious offence against readers, the author whose work is stolen, and the ideals of academic integrity. There are both academic and legal penalties for plagiarism, and these are usually extremely harsh. This is as it should be.

You steal another's ideas or words when you use them in your own work without acknowledging their real source. You commit plagiarism when:

1. You do not make clear exactly what you borrow from a source.
2. You do not make clear exactly who the source is of what you borrow.

You violate the first guideline if (1) you do not enclose verbatim repetition of someone else's wording in quotation marks or (2) you do not plainly distinguish between your own ideas, opinions, and arguments and those of others. You violate the second guideline if you do not properly cite the source of the material you use, even if you don't use the same words.

Using another writer's exact words without enclosing them in quotation marks is the most blatant form of plagiarism. It is a clear-cut violation of the first guideline. You are, however, also guilty of plagiarism if you do not accurately identify the author of an exact quotation even when it is flagged with quotation marks. This error is a violation of the second guideline.

Likewise, you are guilty of plagiarism if you paraphrase or summarize another writer's work without properly citing it. When you paraphrase or summarize, you are not quoting directly, but you are presenting the author's ideas, opinions, or arguments. If you don't acknowledge the author as the source, you are representing the ideas, opinions, or arguments as your own—a violation of the second guideline. You are also guilty of plagiarism if you paraphrase or summarize an author's work, acknowledge the source, but fail to accurately distinguish between the author's ideas and your own—a violation of the first guideline.

One common cause of unintentional plagiarism is a failure to keep careful track of sources consulted. If you read something, take notes and include the source of these notes, even if you don't yet know whether what you've read will be relevant to your paper. It is far too easy to forget which ideas are your own and which came from another source, particularly if it has been a while since you read the original source. Also, even if you remember that you got the idea or words from elsewhere, you might have a difficult time tracking down the reference later.

While plagiarism is the unacknowledged use of someone else's work, it is not considered plagiarism to use material that is considered common knowledge—that is, facts that are well known either in general or among experts in a particular field. There is no sense, for example, in citing anyone as the source of the fact that Immanuel Kant died in 1804, that water freezes at zero degrees Celsius, that a bird in hand is worth two in the bush, or that *modus ponens* is a valid argument form.

Determining what is common knowledge in a particular field can be a challenge for those new to a discipline. In general, if you come across the same facts frequently in an area of study or if they are commonplace information in reference works, you may assume that they are common knowledge. If you aren't sure what you should or should not cite, ask your instructor. If you are still unsure, you should err on the side of caution—citing when it isn't required is far better than failing to cite when it is.

To sum up, plagiarism can take any one of these forms:

- Quoting the author directly (even if just a part of a sentence!) without including both quotation marks and an accurate citation (including page number, if appropriate)
- Paraphrasing or summarizing an argument without citing the source
- Including in paraphrases or summaries some of the author's exact wording without putting it in quotation marks
- Imitating too closely the author's language and style in paraphrases and summaries (a violation even when you cite the source)
- Using the ideas of another (even a fellow student) without acknowledgement

You should be aware that many instructors make use of plagiarism-checking websites such as *Turnitin.com*. This is something that you, as an honest student, should welcome. It acts as a deterrent to potential plagiarists, levelling the field, and maintains the value of a degree from your institution. (There are, of course, additional ways instructors detect plagiarism, whether they use *Turnitin.com* or not.)

### Rule 7-3    Cite Your Sources Carefully

When you cite sources in your paper, you should use a citation, or documentation, system that indicates precisely and consistently who or what your sources are. There are several systems available, and your instructor may require you to use a particular one. Three of them, however, enjoy considerable currency in the humanities, and we will discuss them briefly here. For further information, see Appendix B.

The **documentary-note** (or **humanities**) **system** is the documentation scheme used most in philosophy. This system is given its most detailed and authoritative description in the *Chicago Manual of Style* (CMS).[7] It features superscript (small, raised) numbers in the text that refer to information in footnotes (at the bottom of the page) or in endnotes (at the end of the paper or chapter). Instructors often insist that it be accompanied by a bibliography (see *Rule 7-4*).

Another approach is the **author-page system**, a form of which is recommended by the Modern Language Association (MLA)[8] and by the American Psychological Association.[9] The CMS also outlines a version of it. The method provides some source information in the text itself (for example, author's name and page number) and further, corresponding information in an end-of-paper list usually called "Works Cited" or "References." The text citation may consist of both the author's name and the page number in parentheses, or the author's name mentioned in a sentence of the text with the page number nearby in parentheses.

Appendix B explains how to document sources using the CMS documentary-note system or the MLA or the APA author-page systems. You can find more information about these in the relevant publications.

### Rule 7-4    Build a Bibliography if Needed

A bibliography is a list of sources used in researching and writing a paper. Often instructors ask students to include a bibliography in their papers—even if the papers already have pages of notes.

A bibliography must include all the works cited in the paper, but it also must contain sources consulted but not directly drawn on. Instructors are less likely to ask for a bibliography in a paper using the author-page system of documentation, however, because the list of works cited or references can often do the job. In any case, the final word on whether to include a bibliography must come from your instructor.

*For discussion:*

- Why is plagiarism treated so seriously? Should it be?

- When would you quote instead of summarize or paraphrase? Why?

*For further information:*

- See (again) the recommendations at the end of Chapter 1!

- Familiarize yourself with any reference software available at your institution.

- See Appendix B for information on style conventions.

- If you have questions, ask your instructor *well in advance* of when your paper is due. Don't treat referencing as an afterthought.

# Notes

1.  Rene Descartes, "Meditation II" in *The Philosophical Works of Descartes, Volume I*, trans. Elizabeth Haldane and G.R.T. Ross (Cambridge: Cambridge University Press, 1931), 150.

2.  Richard M. Gale, *On the Nature and Existence of God* (Cambridge: Cambridge University Press, 1991), 238–9.

3.  Philip Kitcher, "Believing Where We Cannot Prove," in *Abusing Science* (Cambridge: MIT Press, 1982), 44.

4.  William K. Frankena, *Ethics*, 2nd ed. (Englewood Cliffs: Prentice-Hall, 1973), 51.

5.  Immanuel Kant, *The Metaphysical Elements of Justice*, trans. John Ladd (Indianapolis: Bobbs-Merrill, 1965), 99–107.

6.  B.F. Skinner, *Beyond Freedom and Dignity* (New York: Bantam, 1971), 17, 19.

7.  *Chicago Manual of Style*, 16th ed. (Chicago: University of Chicago Press, 2010).

8.  *MLA Handbook for Writers of Research Papers*, 7th ed. (New York: MLA, 2009).

9.  *Publication Manual of the American Psychological Association*, 6th ed. (Washington, APA, 2010).

# ❦ PART 2 ❦

# WRITING AND GRAMMAR GUIDE

The following two chapters constitute a brief catalogue of rules for good writing—a quick reference to many of the most common errors and essential skills. Chapter 8 covers the crafting of effective sentences; Chapter 9, the basics of word choice.

If you are serious about improving your writing, this guide should help you—whether you read it straight through from beginning to end or refer to it when you are confronted with a writing problem. If you want to use it as a reference, you can either page through the chapters or scan the book's extended index for a keyword related to a particular writing error or skill. The index includes references to many writing skills, errors, and recommendations.

As this is not primarily a grammar book, we do not dedicate much space to defining basic grammar terms such as *noun, subject,* and *conjunction.* If you are unsure about these words, you may want to keep a dictionary on hand as you read this section. Appendix C also provides further explanation of grammar basics.

Also, if your institution has resources to help students with their writing, use them.

# ❊ 8 ❊

# Writing Effective Sentences

## Rule 8-1  Make the Subject and Verb Agree in Number and Person

A subject and verb must match up in **number** (singular or plural) and **person** (first, second, or third). If they do not agree, the sentence is not only grammatically incorrect but probably confusing and distracting as well.

> Incorrect • The *clerk* do all the paperwork for you.

> Correct • The *clerk does* all the paperwork for you.
> (The subject *clerk* is third person singular and agrees with the verb *does*.)

Do not be confused by plural nouns that separate subject from verb. They do not alter the subject–verb relationship.

> Incorrect • The production of better trucks and of the many gadgets that make driving vehicles easier have changed the market.
> (The subject is *production*, so the verb should be singular—*has changed*, not *have changed*.)

The indefinite pronouns *anyone, everyone, each, each one, someone, everybody, nobody, something, somebody, anything, neither,* and *either* take singular verbs.

> Incorrect • Every boy in the class are doing work.
> Correct • Every boy in the class is doing work.

> Incorrect • Each of them are counting on you.
> Correct • Each of them is counting on you.

Incorrect • Nobody in the platoon shoot straight.
Correct • Nobody in the platoon shoots straight.

The indefinite pronouns *none* and *any*, however, take either a singular or plural verb depending on their referents. If they refer to a singular noun or pronoun, they require a singular verb; if a plural noun or pronoun, a plural verb. (Hint: Regard *none* as singular when it means "no one" or "not one.")

Singular • None is exempt from prosecution.
Plural • None are repaired quickly enough.

Despite appearances to the contrary, a noun in the main part of the sentence does not determine the number of the verb. The subject word determines the number.

Incorrect • The biggest problem are all the trees that block the sun.
Correct • The biggest problem is the trees that block the sun.
Better • The trees that block the sun are the biggest problem.

Incorrect • The tax hikes and the reduction in benefits is a disgrace.
Correct • The tax hikes and the reduction in benefits are a disgrace.

Consider sentences that have this form: ". . . one of the [plural noun] who (or that) + [verb] . . ." For example:

Correct • Ying Ji is one of those people who *work* hard.
(The sentence claims that its subject, Ying Ji, is a member of a group, namely people (plural) who work hard. The verb *work*, therefore, must be plural to agree with *people*.)

In sentences of this form, the verb takes its number from the relative pronoun (*that* or *who*), which is plural because it refers to the plural noun preceding it. The exception to this tenet is that if *the only* precedes *one*, the relative pronoun refers to one, not to the plural noun.

Correct • Sylvie is the only one of my friends who gets A's in school.

In general, when two or more subjects are linked by the word *and*, consider them to be plural and therefore entitled to a plural verb.

Correct • The man's personal philosophy and his lack of income are at odds.

Sometimes two subjects linked by *and* actually refer to a single thing or the same thing. In such cases they should take a singular verb.

Correct • Bacon and eggs is my favourite dish.
Correct • This old soldier and scout is a person of rare courage.

When a subject is singular, it stays singular even when it is coupled with other nouns by phrases such as *along with, as well as, no less than, together with, accompanied by,* and *in addition to.*

Correct • Joshua, as well as Pierre and Hee-Soon, is very cheerful.
Correct • The tide, along with the wind and the rain, was making the trip unbearable.

### Rule 8-2    Express Parallel Ideas in Parallel Form

**Parallelism** is a fundamental principle of good writing. It says that similar ideas should be expressed in similar grammatical structures. Effective parallelism results in sentences that are both well balanced and readable. Lack of parallelism in places where it is needed can yield monstrous sentences and confused readers.

Problems often arise in sentences featuring a series of ideas linked by coordinating conjunctions such as *and, but,* and *or.*

Not Parallel • In school, you should strive for good grades, perfect attendance, and you should have friends.

This series consists of three similar ideas, but its structure is not parallel. It starts with a couple of nouns and ends with a clause. The remedy is to make all three items in the series either nouns or clauses:

Parallel • In school, you should strive for good grades, perfect attendance, and generous friends.

In the following example, we have three similar ideas encased in a non-parallel structure. The first two items in the series are infinitive phrases (that is, they contain a verb in the so-called **infinitive** form: *to go, to run, to help*) but the final one is a noun. Ensuring that all three items are infinitive phrases fixes the problem.

Not Parallel • Juan's goals are to finish high school, to graduate from university, and a job.
Parallel • Juan's goals are to finish high school, to graduate from university, and to get a job.

Paired ideas should also be put in similar form.

Not Parallel • I see that you are both thrifty and are practical.
Parallel • I see that you are both thrifty and practical.

Not Parallel • She is neither a scholar with distinction nor is she a dabbler with curiosity.
Parallel • She is neither a scholar with distinction nor a dabbler with curiosity.

Not Parallel • Camping overnight is better than the prospects of the darkness causing us to lose our way.
Parallel • Camping overnight is better than losing our way in the dark.

## Rule 8-3    Write in Complete Sentences, Not Fragments

A **sentence** is a group of words that comprise a subject and verb and that can stand alone (that is, function as an independent clause). A **sentence fragment** is a group of words that looks like a sentence but is, in fact, merely part of a sentence. Here are a few fragments ensconced with some complete sentences (the fragments are underlined).

Fragment • I decided to ride my bicycle into town. Because my car was out of gas.

Fragment • Angelique says she will never go to another football game. Although many of her friends think that she likes the game.

Fragment • The government may be fooling us with dirty tricks. Such as pretending to care about taxpayers while plotting to raise taxes.

Fragment • I was able to do a lot of research at the library. <u>Going through just about every journal in the field.</u>

You can get rid of a fragment in your writing by (1) deleting it (the most obvious solution), (2) attaching it to a complete sentence, or (3) turning it into a complete sentence. For example:

Fragment • The government may be fooling us with dirty tricks. <u>Pretending to care about taxpayers while plotting to raise taxes.</u>
Attached to a Sentence • The government may be fooling us with dirty tricks, pretending to care about taxpayers while plotting to raise taxes.
Turned into a Sentence • The government may be fooling us with dirty tricks. It may be pretending to care about taxpayers while plotting to raise taxes.

From time to time, even the best writers use fragments. They use them sparingly, however, and only for good reasons (such as to add emphasis). Inexperienced writers should avoid using fragments in their academic writing unless they too have good reasons, which is usually not the case.

## Rule 8-4    Connect Independent Clauses Properly

Sometimes inexperienced writers jam two independent clauses together without connecting them correctly. The result is a run-on sentence.

Run-on • Kathryn cleaned the office from top to bottom she wasn't finished until the end of the day.

Run-on • Politicians never seem to tell the truth, how can they live with themselves?

Run-on • I knew Aziz was there, I could see his head half-hidden by the curtain.

The first example is a kind of run-on called a **fused sentence**. It forces two independent clauses together without any punctuation or connecting word at all. The other two examples are called **comma splices** because the clauses are joined by just a comma when a much stronger or clearer connection is required. You can easily mend these errors, but the fix depends on what meaning you want to convey.

You can repair the fused sentence by joining the two clauses with both a comma and a coordinating conjunction (*and, or, but, for, yet,* or *so*). The comma always goes in front of the conjunction.

Repaired • Kathryn cleaned the office from top to bottom, and she wasn't finished until the end of the day.

You can achieve a similar effect by joining the clauses with a semi-colon. In this kind of construction, no coordinating conjunction is necessary.

Repaired • Kathryn cleaned the office from top to bottom; she wasn't finished until the end of the day.

You can be more specific about the relationship between the two clauses by adding a conjunctive adverb such as *however, consequently,* or *therefore* after the semicolon.

Repaired • Kathryn cleaned the office from top to bottom; therefore, she wasn't finished until the end of the day.

In each of these revisions the two clauses are given more or less equal weight, with neither seeming to be more important than the other. Another approach, however, is to subordinate one of the clauses to the other.

Repaired • Because Kathryn cleaned the office from top to bottom, she wasn't finished until the end of the day.

Perhaps the most obvious option is to change the paired clauses into two distinct sentences.

Repaired • Kathryn cleaned the office from top to bottom. She wasn't finished until the end of the day.

You can modify the two comma splices, of course, in much the same way. The first one is composed of a declarative statement and a question, so the most plausible way to change it is to turn it into two sentences.

Repaired • Politicians never seem to tell the truth. How can they live with themselves?

At first you may consider correcting the second comma splice by adding a coordinating conjunction after the comma. You can achieve a more natural reading, however, by turning the clauses into separate sentences, joining them with a semicolon, or subordinating one of the clauses.

Repaired • I knew Aziz was there; I could see his head half-hidden by the curtain.
Repaired • I knew Aziz was there because I could see his head half-hidden by the curtain.

## Rule 8-5    Delete the Deadwood

Wordiness is the use of more words than necessary to express your meaning. When you use 20 words to convey an idea that can be expressed easily in 10, you are being wordy. You are packing your writing with deadwood—needless words that merely fill space. Wordiness is measured not by how many words you use, but by how many *excess* words. Consider this passage:

In light of the fact that an appreciable number of employed workers are exceeding their allotted allowance of excess working hours, it is necessary that for the time being excess hours must be suspended by the manager until such time as the plant can be updated to better and more modern equipment.

Now compare it to this version:

Because many employees are working too much overtime, the manager must temporarily suspend it until we can modernize the plant.

These two sentences mean almost the same thing. The first one, however, uses 52 words to say it; the second one, 20 words. The first is inefficient, hard to understand, stilted, and dull. The second one is far more concise, easier to grasp, and more vigorous. Readers would rather read a whole page of such economical writing than one paragraph of bloated, windy prose.

A common cause of wordiness is deadwood expressions—long phrases with meanings that could be stated in a mere word or two. All the following phrases have a concise substitute.

| Deadwood | Substitute |
|---|---|
| by means of | by |
| in a bold manner | boldly |
| in order to | to |
| due to the fact that | because |
| have an effect upon | affect |
| in spite of the fact that | though, although |
| at the present time | now, currently |
| she is a woman who | she |
| because of the fact that | because |
| until such time as | until |
| for the purpose of | to |
| in the event that | if |
| give consideration to | consider |

## Rule 8-6    Put Modifiers in Their Place

**Modifiers** are words, phrases, or clauses that act as adjectives or adverbs. If you position modifiers incorrectly, confusion or hilarity may result. If you place them properly, the reader will have no doubts about which word they modify, and your meaning will be clear.

In their writing, students often misplace modifying phrases and clauses. For example:

Misplaced • Theo tried to change the tire while the rain was pouring down in a fit of rage.
Improved • In a fit of rage, Theo tried to change the tire while the rain was pouring down.

The remedy here is to position the modifying phrase "in a fit of rage" closer to the word modified—"Theo."

Misplaced • He saw that the lights were off in the cabin while standing under a tree.
Improved • While standing under a tree, he saw that the lights were off in the cabin.

Who or what was standing under a tree? The confusion is cleared up after moving "while standing under a tree" in front of "he."

Misplaced • There is a flower in her apartment that smells like onions.
Improved • In her apartment, there is a flower that smells like onions.

Relative clauses (such as "that smells like onions") should usually follow immediately after their antecedents. "Flower" is the antecedent here, so the relative clause comes after it.

When a modifier appears in a sentence without a word to modify, it is said to be **dangling**. Showing up often in student writing, dangling modifiers are sometimes hilarious and always either perplexing or distracting. Typically they appear as phrases at the start of a sentence and pretend to modify the word that immediately follows.

Incorrect • Before shooting again, the squirrel fell near the hunter.
Correct • Before shooting again, the hunter saw the squirrel fall nearby.

Incorrect • After loosening his tie and kicking off his shoes, the feather bed was the only thing Harry had on his mind.
Correct • After loosening his tie and kicking off his shoes, Harry could think only of the feather bed.

Incorrect • To keep the students happy, the windows were opened.
Correct • To keep the students happy, we opened the windows.

Some words modify other words by restricting or limiting their meaning: for example, *only*, *even*, *nearly*, and *almost*. Unfortunately, when these adverbs are not inserted immediately before the words they modify, they become misplaced modifiers.

Incorrect • I only learned of her illness yesterday.
Correct • I learned of her illness only yesterday.

Incorrect • The government has determined that the rations should be only distributed to the neediest people.
Correct • The government has determined that the rations should be distributed to only the neediest people.

Incorrect • I nearly spent all the money.
Correct • I spent nearly all the money.

## Rule 8-7   Be Consistent in Tense, Voice, Number, and Person

If you begin writing with one grammatical structure then shift unnecessarily to another, you may confuse (or annoy) your reader. In sentences and paragraphs, you should stay with one tense, voice, number, and person unless you have a good reason for shifting.

Shifted • I walked past the front desk and into the stacks of the library. When I got to the philosophy section, I see a whole shelf of books about Kant. I stopped in my tracks.

This description of action begins in past tense then suddenly drops into present tense in the second sentence and back again to the past in the third. Making the tenses consistent throughout rectifies the problem.

Consistent • I walked past the front desk and into the stacks of the library. When I got to the philosophy section, I saw a whole shelf of books about Kant. I stopped in my tracks.

In philosophical writing, the convention is to discuss or summarize a philosopher's work in present tense. The events of a philosopher's life, however, are usually described in past tense.

Correct • In ordinary circumstances, however, the self seems to be unified, and any process theory must account for this apparent unity of the self. Immanuel Kant (1724–1804) accounts for it by postulating a "transcendental ego" that lies behind our experience and structures it according to certain rules. Kant's self is transcendental because it cannot be directly observed.[1]

Careful writers ensure that pronouns and nouns are consistent in person (*I*, *you*, *he/she*, *we*, *you*, *they*) within a sentence or paragraph.

Shifted • Students must keep up with homework or you will fall behind in both your homework and tests.

This sentence begins in third person (*students*) but switches to second person (*you, your*) in the second clause. The solution is to stick with either third or second person throughout the sentence.

> Consistent • Students must keep up with homework, or they will fall behind in both homework and tests.
> Consistent • You must keep up with homework, or you will fall behind in both homework and tests.

Now consider this shift from first person to second:

> Shifted • I was frightened as I walked past the graveyard because shadows can play tricks on your mind.
> Consistent • I was frightened as I walked past the graveyard because shadows kept playing tricks on my mind.

## Rule 8-8    Communicate Pronoun References Clearly

Pronouns are supposed to refer to specific words—to nouns, the antecedents of the pronouns. These references must be clear, or else readers will get sidetracked while trying to trace the path from pronoun to corresponding noun. A pronoun should refer to a particular word, not to a vague or general idea or to a word that is merely implied but not stated.

A common problem is the use of *this, that, which,* and *it* to refer not to a particular antecedent but to something more vague—a whole sentence or some blurry, unspoken notion.

> Vague Reference • Nandini had a quick lunch then went for a long walk. This made her too tired to do any reading.

To what does *This* refer? Here the reference is clear:

> Clear Reference • Nandini had a quick lunch then went for a long walk. The walk made her too tired to do any reading.

> Vague Reference • Fodor is a physicalist and a non-reductionist, which puts him at odds with identity theorists.
> Clear Reference • Like identity theorists, Fodor is a physicalist. It is his non-reductionism that puts him at odds with identity theorists.

**Vague Reference** • In Frankena's *Ethics*, it shows that moral theories have many subtypes.
**Clear Reference** • In *Ethics*, Frankena shows that moral theories have many subtypes.

Vague references using *they* are particularly prevalent but can be easily corrected.

**Vague Reference** • They are trying to provide more beds for the homeless.
**Clear Reference** • City councillors are trying to provide more beds for the homeless.

Sometimes a pronoun's referent is unclear because of ambiguity—the pronoun could stand for either of two antecedents. (See Chapter 3 for more on ambiguity.)

**Ambiguous Reference** • Sharon was listening to the radio in her car when it suddenly stopped functioning.
**Clear Reference** • Sharon was listening to the radio in her car when the engine suddenly stopped running.

The antecedent of a pronoun must actually be contained in a sentence, not merely implied by the sentence's content. Consider the following:

**Implied Reference** • Thomas Aquinas's first-cause argument has some defects that he never recognized.

Here, the writer might believe a reader ought to figure out that Aquinas did not recognize *any* of the defects in the first-cause argument. The conventions of grammar, however, allow for the interpretation that Aquinas knew about plenty of the defects, and was only ignorant of *some*. The following version avoids the problem:

**Clear Reference** • Thomas Aquinas never recognized the defects in his first-cause argument.

# Note

1.  Theodore Schick, Jr., and Lewis Vaughn, *Doing Philosophy: An Introduction through Thought Experiments* (New York: McGraw-Hill, 2003), 277.

# ❦ 9 ❦
# Choosing the Right Words

### Rule 9-1  Select Nouns and Verbs Precisely

Sometimes writers are imprecise and wordy because they try to modify every noun and verb with an adjective or adverb. Carefully chosen nouns and verbs, however, often do not need to be modified. You need not write *walked slowly and clumsily* when *lumbered* will do, or *speak very softly* when *whisper* is fine, or *wrote hastily* when *jotted* is fitting. Likewise you have nothing to gain by writing *large house* if *mansion* will suffice, or *upper limb* when you mean *arm*.

### Rule 9-2  Prefer the Active Voice

In **active voice**, the subject does the action (*Kim drove the car*); in **passive voice**, the subject receives the action (*The car was driven by Kim*). Both constructions have their uses. Passive voice is appropriate when you want to focus on the receiver of the action or when the doer of the action cannot or should not be identified (for example, *The jewels were stolen last night*). In general, you should prefer the active voice in all other cases. Compared to passive voice, active voice is often more concise, more direct, and more vigorous.

Passive Voice • The mountainside was crashed into by the meteor.
Active Voice • The meteor crashed into the mountainside.

Passive Voice • That all our knowledge derives from experience was maintained by the empiricists—who are best represented by the British philosophers Locke, Berkeley, and Hume.
Active Voice • The empiricists (for example, British philosophers Locke, Berkeley, and Hume) argued that all knowledge derives from experience.

## Rule 9-3    Use Specific Terms

General words refer to entire categories of things: *parent, vegetation, colour, male, fast*. Specific words refer to particular or definite examples of such categories: *Whistler's mother, the grass on your lawn, that shade of red, Sartre, 90 kilometres per hour*. In some circumstances, a general word is best; in other instances, a more specific word works better. Good writers, however, strive to be as specific as a given context will allow. They know that specific terms often convey more information more vividly than general terms do.

General • She travelled back to her residence due to adverse weather.
Specific • Anne took a taxi back to her high-rise apartment because a snowstorm was pounding the city.

General • This moral theory forbids actions that can cause harm.
Specific • This moral theory, a consequentialist view, forbids actions that can cause physical pain to other people or put them at greater risk of experiencing physical pain.

## Rule 9-4    Avoid Redundancy

A characteristic of writing that can increase wordiness and reduce clarity is redundancy—pointlessly expressing the same idea twice. Redundancy, which frequently arises in common phrases, suggests carelessness and ignorance of word meanings. Substitute concise terms for redundant ones.

| Redundant | Not Redundant |
| --- | --- |
| true facts | facts |
| refer back | refer |
| future forecast | forecast |
| mix together | mix |
| few in number | few |
| free gift | gift |
| advance planning | planning |
| connect together | connect |

## Rule 9-5    Be Aware of the Connotations of Words

A large part of making appropriate word choices is understanding the connotations of words. Connotations are the feelings or attitudes associated with a word or phrase—associations beyond the literal meaning of the term. Consider these word pairs:

| | |
|---|---|
| retreat | strategic withdrawal |
| intellectual | egghead |
| sweat | perspire |
| prank | vandalism |
| collateral damage | civilian casualties |
| psychiatrist | shrink |
| downsized | fired |
| guerrillas | freedom fighters |

The words in each pair refer to the same object or state of affairs, but the images or emotions conveyed are dramatically different.

To write well, you must be aware of both the literal meaning of words and their connotations. You must also understand that people often use connotations to put an argument or view in a negative or positive light in a way that may be misleading or partisan. In debates about abortion, for example, those who oppose abortion may refer to their position as "pro-life" or "pro-child." Those opposed to this view may call it "anti-choice" or even "anti-woman." In disputes about gun ownership, those who want to restrict gun ownership may label their position as "against assault weapons." Those opposed to this position may call it "against self-defence." Such labels are intended to provoke particular attitudes toward the subject matter—attitudes that may not be justified by any evidence or argument.

Words used to convey positive or neutral attitudes or emotions in place of more negative ones are known as euphemisms (for example, *neutralize* for *kill*). Words used to convey negative attitudes or emotions in place of neutral or positive ones are sometimes called dysphemisms (*dive* for *tavern*). Both euphemisms and dysphemisms can mislead. As a critical reader, you should be on guard against the deceptive use of connotations. As a critical writer, you should rely primarily on argument and evidence to make your case.

Remember, however, that euphemisms often serve legitimate purposes by allowing people to discuss sensitive subjects in an unobjectionable way. You may spare a person's feelings by saying that his loved one "has passed" or "passed on" rather than "has died," or that her dog was "put to sleep" rather than "killed."

### Rule 9-6    Learn to Distinguish Words That Writers Frequently Mix Up

**adverse**: contrary to, opposed to
**averse**: disinclined, ill-disposed to

**affect**: *v.* to influence; *n.* emotion
**effect**: *v.* to accomplish; *n.* result

**allusion**: indirect or veiled reference
**illusion**: faulty perception, delusion

**beside**: near
**besides**: apart from, also

**compliment**: *n.* praise; *v.* to praise
**complement**: *n.* counterpart, supplement; *v.* to complete or supplement

**comprise**: to include or consist of (the whole *comprises* the parts)
**compose**: to make up (the parts *compose* the whole)

**continuous**: occurring uninterrupted, unceasing
**continual**: frequently recurring, occurring intermittently

**disinterested**: impartial
**uninterested**: not interested

**ensure**: make sure, guarantee
**insure**: buy or give financial insurance

**farther**: at a greater *physical* distance
**further**: at a greater figurative distance (for example, "we discussed the issue further")

**flout**: to express contempt for
**flaunt**: to show off

**fortuitous:** happening by chance
**fortunate:** lucky

**imminent:** happening soon, impending
**eminent:** notable, distinguished

**infer:** to deduce
**imply:** to suggest

**lay:** to place (for example, "he lay the book down")
**lie:** *v.* to recline; past tense is *lay* (for example, "I *lie* on the bed, just as I *lay* on the bed yesterday")

**like:** *prep.* similar to [a noun or noun phrase] (for example, "she looks like Karen")
**as:** *conj.* similar to [verbs or clauses] (for example, "she looks as if she ran a mile")

**literally:** actually; in the literal sense of the word; without figurative language
**figuratively:** metaphorically; in the figurative sense; not literally

**oral:** spoken
**verbal:** having to do with words

**principal:** *adj.* chief, main; *n.* head of a school
**principle:** *n.* basic truth, law, doctrine

## Rule 9-7    Strive for Freshness; Avoid Clichés

A cliché is an overused, stale expression—the kind you should try to avoid in all your writing. Clichés were once fresh and interesting ways of expressing an idea. Overuse, however, drained the life out of them. *Blind as a bat, busy as a bee, playing with fire, light as a feather, saved by the bell, water over the dam*—these and many other trite expressions show up in student writing frequently. They signal to readers that the writer is not putting much original thought into the composition. Even worse, they prevent writers from thinking for themselves and achieving a novel perspective.

Clichés, of course, can sometimes help you say something accurately. You should, however, avoid them when you can; instead, express your ideas literally, or use metaphors that are original or especially effective in the context.

## Rule 9-8    Do Not Mix Metaphors

Metaphors can be extremely effective in compositions. Using metaphorical language well, however, is not easy, and you should not attempt it unless you are confident of the results. Most of the time, using no metaphors is better than concocting metaphors that are poorly made or confused.

A problem common in student papers is the mixed metaphor—a mixture of images that do not fit well together. Alone, each image may convey a coherent idea, but together the images form a ludicrous, even impossible, picture.

> Mixed • In this administration, the ship of state has thrown in the towel on affirmative action and marched to the beat of a different drummer.

The clash of these incongruent images is distracting, confusing, and laughable. If there ever was a serious point here, the mixed metaphor killed it. (In addition to the images being mixed, the expressions are clichés.)

The best way to avoid mixed metaphors (and most other misuses of metaphorical language) is to try to visualize the image you create. If your visualization reveals a coherent, apt picture, then your metaphor may be acceptable. If your picture is defective, revision or deletion is in order.

## Rule 9-9    Beware of Awkward Repetition

When handled carefully, the repetition of words can achieve emphasis, cohesion, and emotive force. Clumsy repetition, however, offends the ear and signals an inexperienced hand.

> Awkward Repetition • We are studying so we might understand more about Spinoza and understand his main ideas.

> Awkward Repetition • As soon as you do the analysis on the projections, you can check the analysis against the files.

> Awkward Repetition • He could see that two ducks were on the pond, three ducks were on the dock, and five ducks were missing.

**Effective Repetition** • Next to the enormous war and the massive landscape and the huge sky, she seemed ever so small, with small hands clutching her small child, living in a small village in a small shack, which held a small bag containing everything she had.

**Effective Repetition** • "We shall go on to the end. We shall fight in France, we shall fight on the seas and oceans, we shall fight with growing confidence and growing strength in the air, we shall defend our island, whatever the cost may be. We shall fight on the beaches, we shall fight on the landing grounds, we shall fight in the fields and in the streets, we shall fight in the hills; we shall never surrender..."[1]

# Note

1.    Winston Churchill, speech to House of Commons of the Parliament of the United Kingdom, June 4, 1940.

# ❧ Appendix A ❧

# Formatting Your Paper

The formatting conventions discussed here are commonly used in the humanities and are consistent with the general guidelines in *The Chicago Manual of Style* (CMS). (Referencing conventions for CMS, and also for two other styles, are discussed in further detail in Appendix B.) Most instructors are tolerant of stylistic variations, but be sure to ask if you are not clear on the requirements. The formatting preferences of your instructor, of course, trump anything in this appendix.

## General Specifications

- Use good-quality paper (neither onion-skin thickness nor card stock), "letter" size (8½ × 11 inches or 216 × 279 mm), white.
- Use a 12-point standard font such as Times New Roman or Arial, both common word-processing fonts.
- Ensure that there are margins of at least one inch at the top, bottom, and sides of the page. Double-space the text.
- Number all pages consecutively, starting with 1, and insert the numbers in the upper-right corner of each page. The first page is the title page. Do not show the page number on the title page. The first visible page number should appear on the next page—page 2. (Alternatively, and often preferable if you are submitting the body of your paper to a site such as turnitin.com, have your title page be a different file. Then, the body of your paper starts on page 1. In this case, both the title page and the first actual body page do not list page numbers.)
- If your instructor wants you to include an abstract (a very succinct characterization of your paper), one common convention is to include it at the top of the first page, single-spaced, italicized, and centre justified with wider margins. Like this:

> I argue that, of the two standard conceptions of biological function, the systems theoretic is more fundamental than the

etiological on the grounds that performance is prior to continued performance. I consider the objection that systems theoretic biological functions have no explanatory role (and hence no role in biology) and reject it.

- On the title page, centre (1) the full title of your essay, (2) your name and student number, (3) the title of the course, (4) your instructor's name, and (5) the date. If other information is relevant (e.g., class section), be sure to include it.

Utilitarianism and Our Considered Moral Judgments

The Divine Command Theory
and God's Moral Character

Nadia Markovic

Philosophy 233: Introduction to Ethics
Professor Cheng
15 October 2009

2

*An abstract would go here. It should be obvious to the reader that it is an abstract, and when the body of the paper starts. Your thesis should be clear. It is not unusual to use parts of the abstract, or even the whole thing, in the introductory paragraph of the body. You should act as though the reader has not read the abstract.*

Many people believe that God is a lawgiver who alone defines what actions are right and wrong. God, in other words, is the author of morality; an action is right if and only if God commands it to be done. According to this view, there is no right or wrong until God says so, and nothing is moral or immoral independently of God's willing it to be thus. God, and only God, *makes* rightness and wrongness. This view is known as the divine command theory of morality.

A simple version of the theory is widely accepted today, among both the religious and non-religious. In this version, God is thought to be the source of all moral principles and values. He can be the source of all morality because he is omnipotent, being able to do anything whatsoever, including create the very foundations of right and wrong.

In the *Euthyphro*, Socrates brings out what is probably the oldest and strongest criticism of the theory. He asks, in effect, is an action right because God commands it to be done, or does God command it to be done because it is right? This question lays bare the dilemma that is inherent in the theory: If an action is right because God commands it, then there is nothing in the action itself that makes it right, and God's command is arbitrary. If God commands the action because it is right (that is,

## Quotations and Citations

- Block quotes are usually separated from regular text by leaving a blank line before and after the block quote and by indenting the left edge of the block quote four or five spaces.
- Start endnotes on their own page. Number the endnote pages along with the rest of the pages. Centre the word "Notes" at the top of the page. Indent endnotes as shown in Appendix B.
- Single-space each endnote. Insert one line space between entries.
- On a separate page, start a list of the works to which your paper has referred. Number the pages with the rest of the paper. Centre the words "Works Cited" at the top of the page. Indent entries as shown in Appendix B.
- Double-space each line of Works Cited notes.
- Use a "Notes" page from Appendix B as a model for the spacing in a bibliography. Start a bibliography on its own page. Number the pages along with the rest of the paper. Indent a bibliography as you would a Works Cited page (*Rule 7-4*).

5

If a prediction turns out to be false, we can always save the
hypothesis by modifying the background theory. As Philip
Kitcher notes:

> Individual scientific claims do not, and cannot, confront
> the evidence one by one. Rather . . . "hypotheses are tested
> in bundles." . . . We can only test relatively large bundles
> of claims. What this means is that when our experiments
> go awry we are not logically compelled to select any
> particular claim as the culprit. We can always save a
> cherished hypothesis from refutation by rejecting (however
> implausibly) one of the other members of the bundle. Of
> course, this is exactly what I did in the illustration of Newton
> and the apple above. Faced with disappointing results, I
> suggested that we could abandon the (tacit) additional claim
> that no large forces besides gravity were operating on the
> apple. . . . Creationists can appeal to naive falsification
> to show that evolution is not a science. But, given the
> traditional picture of theory and evidence I have sketched,
> one can appeal to naive falsification to show that *any* science
> is not a science.[4]

To see this point, let's examine Christopher Columbus's
claim that the Earth is round. Both Christopher Columbus
and Nicholas Copernicus rejected the flat Earth hypothesis on
the grounds that its predictions were contrary to experience.

7

Notes

1. Alasdair MacIntyre, *A Short History of Ethics*, 2nd ed. (New York: Macmillan, 1998), 178–79.

2. Brooke Noel Moore and Kenneth Bruder, *Philosophy: The Power of Ideas*, 6th ed. (New York: McGraw Hill, 2005), 285.

3. Joel Feinberg, ed., *Reason and Responsibility* (Belmont, CA: Wadsworth, 1981), 430.

4. MacIntyre, 190.

5. Moore and Bruder, 411.

6. John Scott, review of Limits of Imagination, by Samantha Speers, *American Journal of Imaginative Studies* 10 (1990): 321–34.

7. Peter Suber, *Guide to Philosophy on the Internet*, February 16, 2003, http://www.earlham.edul~peters/philinks.htm (accessed September 7, 2009).

8. Saul Traiger, "Hume on Finding an Impression of the Self," *Hume Studies* 11, no. 1 (April 1985), http://www.humesociety.org/hs/issues/v11n1/traiger/traiger-v11n1.pdf (accessed September 10, 2009).

9. James Rachels, "The Challenge of Cultural Relativism," in *Ethics: History, Theory, and Contemporary Issues*, 4th ed., ed. Steven M. Cahn and Peter Markie (New York: Oxford University Press, 2009), 633–39.

10. MacIntyre, 234.

11. Traiger.

12. John R. Searle, "Minds, Brains, and Programs," *Behavioral and Brain Sciences* 3 (1980): 417–24.

9

Works Cited

Fisher, Johnna, ed. *Biomedical Ethics: A Canadian Focus*. Don
Mills, ON: Oxford University Press, 2009.

Johnson, Larry. *The Ancient Greeks*. 7th ed. New York: Putnam-
Bantam, 2003.

– – – . *The Hellenic Age*. 5th ed. New York: Oxford-Putnam, 2005.

MacIntyre, Alasdair. *After Virtue*. Indianapolis: Notre Dame, 1984.
http://www.luc.edu.depts/philosophy/tec/eac6/macintyre-
tradition.pdf (accessed October 1, 2009).

Rachels, James. "The Challenge of Cultural Relativism." In
*Ethics: History, Theory, and Contemporary Issues*, 4th ed.,
edited by Steven M. Cahn and Peter Markie. New York:
Oxford University Press, 2009.

Simpson, Carol. *Time's Arrow: The Ancient Conceptions of Time,
Motion, and Symmetry*. Mountain View: Upton, 1980.

Smith, Nancy H., et al. *Philosophy, Mathematics, and Mysticism in
Ancient Times*. 5th ed. Mountain View: Greenland, 1967.

Suber, Peter. *Guide to Philosophy on the Internet*. February
16, 2003. http://www.earlham.edu/~peters/philinks.htm
(accessed September 7, 2009).

Traiger, Saul. "Hume on Finding an Impression of the Self." *Hume
Studies* 11, no. 1 (April 1985), http://www.humesociety.
org/hs/issues/v11n1/traiger/traiger-v11n1.pdf (accessed
September 10, 2009).

# ❦ Appendix B ❦
# Documenting Your Sources

The first thing to keep in mind is that the point of documenting your sources is to give your reader enough information to enable him or her to find the works you consulted. It is important to follow the conventions laid out for you in class, but most instructors would rather you provide more information than required instead of less. Not only does doing so make the works easier to locate (imagine your reader thinking "Wow! That sounds really interesting—I'd love to read that whole paper"), it can help you to avoid any problems with plagiarism or the appearance of plagiarism. (See Chapter 7 for more discussion on plagiarism.)

You could profit greatly from checking out what documentation resources are available through your library. There are quite a few software options to make gathering and formatting references easier.

We look at three different styles of documentation in this appendix: CMS (*The Chicago Manual of Style*), MLA (Modern Language Association), and APA (American Psychological Association).

## The CMS Documentary-Note System

Full information about this documentation style is available in *The Chicago Manual of Style*, 16th ed. (Chicago: University of Chicago Press, 2010). Another useful source is the online Chicago-Style Citation Quick Guide (www.chicagomanualofstyle.org/tools_citationguide.html).

In this approach, note numbers are inserted into the text in superscript, in consecutive order, after all punctuation marks (but not the dash), and at the end of the relevant text passage. (See the note numbers in the quoted passages throughout this book.) Each note number, of course, refers to a corresponding reference note, which may be treated as a footnote or endnote. If the notes are treated as footnotes, they are placed in numerical order at the bottom of the page on which the corresponding note numbers appear. If they are treated as endnotes, they are gathered together in a numerically ordered list at the end of the paper under the heading "Notes."

Reference notes must contain all relevant publication information so that readers can easily find sources for review or study. To ensure that the information is accessible and useful to readers, the notes must consistently follow a specified format, which varies depending what kind of source is being cited. The first time a source is cited in a note, the note must include a full citation—that is, all the required information (author's name, title of publication, city and year of publication, publisher, etc.) in the proper order. All later reference notes for the same source should be abbreviated and, in the case of books, may consist of just the author's last name and a page number (for example, Johnson, 99). Later notes referring to multiple works by the same author should also be abbreviated but include a condensed version of the work's title (for example, Johnson, *Greeks and Ancient*, 153 [refers to a book]; or Johnson, "Ideas Rising," 340 [refers to an article]).

The following sections illustrate the proper CMS note format for the first full reference of several different types of sources. Notice that the usual sequence of information for a simple note is name of author or authors; title of the book (or article plus journal name); city of publication; name of publisher; year of publication; page number(s).

## Books

To find a book's publication information, look at the title page first then the copyright page. See note 1 below for an example of how subsequent references to the same book are shortened.

*One author:*

1.    Alasdair MacIntyre, *A Short History of Ethics* (New York: Macmillan, 1998), 178–9.

[Note: Book title is always italicized or underlined.]

*Subsequent reference to same book:*

33.    MacIntyre, 165.

*Subsequent reference to another book by same author includes abbreviated title:*

47.    MacIntyre, *After Virtue*, 104.

[Note: This format only gets used when the article's full title and source has been provided in an earlier citation.]

**Two or three authors**

2.   Leo A. Groarke and Christopher W. Tindale, *Good Reasoning Matters! A Constructive Approach to Critical Thinking*, 4th ed. (Don Mills, ON: Oxford University Press, 2008), 285.

3.   Stanley M. Honer, Thomas C. Hunt, and Dennis L. Okholm, *Invitation to Philosophy* (Belmont, CA: Wadsworth, 1992), 49–52.

**More than three authors:**

4.   Greg Bassham et al., *Critical Thinking: A Student's Introduction* (Boston: McGraw-Hill, 2002), 155.

**Editor, translator, or compiler but no author:**

5.   Johnna Fisher, ed., *Biomedical Ethics: A Canadian Focus* (Don Mills, ON: Oxford University Press, 2009), 363.

6.   Gerald Forbes and Nina Johnson, trans., *Prose from the North Country* (Dayton, OH: Ingram and Consetti, 1989), 342.

7.   Gregory Knopf, comp. *Complete Papers of Nonia Forge* (London: Hutton Kind, 1949), 347.

**Editor, translator, or compiler with an author:**

8.   Edgar Eddington, *Edge of Night*, ed. Maureen Dodd (Buffalo, NY: Tiffton Press, 1966), 213.

[Note: Author's name first; editor, translator, compiler name after title.]

**No author:**

9.   *Bound for Glory* (Eugene: Winston-Hane, 1976), 343.

**Later editions:**

10.   Irving M. Copi and Carl Cohen, *Introduction to Logic*, 9th ed. (New York: Macmillan, 1994), 109.

**Chapter in a book:**

11.   Norman Melchert, "Nature Philosophers," in *The Great Conversation* (Mountain View, CA: Mayfield, 1991), 7–15.

**Essay in an anthology:**

12.   James Rachels, "The Challenge of Cultural Relativism," in *Ethics: History, Theory, and Contemporary Issues*, ed. Steven M. Cahn and Peter Markie (New York: Oxford University Press, 2009), 633.

*Preface, foreword, or introduction:*

13. John Smith, introduction to *Reason and Rhetoric,* by Theodore Thomas (New York: Warrington Press, 1966), 89.

[Note: Author of introduction mentioned first; author of book itself follows title.]

*Specific volume in a multivolume set:*

14. Thomas Kane, *The Issues of the 21st Century,* vol. 5, *The Issues of History* (New York: Warrington Press, 1955), 222.

[Note: Citation refers to whole volume.]

15. Thomas Kane, *The Issues of History* (New York: Warrington Press, 1955), 4:125–40.

[Note: This format is used when the volume title is not given. Citation refers to volume 4 and page numbers 125–40.]

*Entire multivolume set:*

16. Mary Ingram, ed., *International Law and Commerce,* 4 vols. (London: Greenland Press, 1951).

*Corporate author:*

17. National Literature Council, *Literature in the Classroom* (New York: National Literature Council, 2001).

## Periodicals

*Journal article:*

18. John R. Searle, "Minds, Brains, and Programs," *Behavioral and Brain Sciences* 3 (1980): 417–24.

[Note: Citation indicates volume 3, publication date of 1980, and pages 417–24. Article titles are always enclosed in quotation marks; journal names are always in italics or underlined. For journals whose page numbers run consecutively from the beginning of the year to the end through all issues (that is, all pages are in the same volume), the volume number, page numbers, and year are sufficient for identification, as in the example here. For journals whose page numbers start at page 1 in each issue, both volume number and issue number must be cited. For example: *Behavioral and Brain Sciences* 3, no. 4 (1980): 417–24. The volume number is 3; the issue number, 4.]

19.  Edmund L. Gettier, "Is Justified True Belief Knowledge?" *Analysis* 23 (1963): 121–23.

[Note: No comma is required after the article title when the title ends in a question mark or exclamation point.]

*Subsequent reference to same article:*

32.  Searle, 420.

*Subsequent reference to another article by same author includes abbreviated article title:*

40.  Searle, "Is the Brain's Mind," 420.

[Note: This format only gets used when the article's full title and source has been provided in an earlier citation.]

*Magazine article:*

20.  Allan Casey, "Rocking the Boat," *Canadian Geographic*, June 2011, 60–6.

[Note: Includes month and year in date without an intervening comma.]

21.  Seymour M. Hersh, "Annals of National Security: The Iran Game," *New Yorker*, December 3, 2001, 42–50.

[Note: Day of the month follows the month with a comma separating the date from the year.]

*Book review:*

22.  John Scott, review of *Limits of Imagination*, by Samantha Speers, *American Journal of Imaginative Studies* 10 (1990): 321–34.

[Note: Author of review is mentioned first; author of book is stated after book title.]

23.  Nicholas Lemann, "Pure Act," review of *Theodore Rex*, by Edmund Morris, *New Yorker*, November 19, 2001, 81–4.

*Newspaper article:*

24. David Jackson, "The Rise in Crime," *Buffalo Eagle-News,* November 3, 2003, late edition.

[Note: Page numbers are not included.]

25. Editorial, *Buffalo Eagle-News,* November 3, 2003, late edition.
26. "Edward Jones, Dead at 86," *Buffalo Eagle-News,* November 3, 2003, late edition.

[Note: No author mentioned.]

## Online Works

The CMS style recommends that citations for resources accessed online include, in addition to the usual data, information that can lead the reader directly to the item. A generic name for an identifier is an *accession number.* This is any number (or set of symbols) that uniquely picks out the item in question. ISBNs (for books) play the same function (though no standard citation system currently requires listing ISBNs). They are permanent and unique "names" for the item in question.

On the Internet, an identifier is, typically, either a URL (uniform resource locator) or a DOI (digital object identifier). A URL is what is commonly thought of as an address—it is what you would paste into your browser to get to the site where the work is posted or otherwise available. For example, http://www.chicagomanualofstyle.org is the URL for *The Chicago Manual of Style.*

One problem with URLs is that they are not always stable, meaning that they might cease to be the right address for the item. Enter the DOI. This is effectively a permanent name for a particular piece of intellectual property in whatever medium, though it is used most often with works stored electronically. To find the object, enter its DOI at http://dx.doi.org.

The following sample notes conform to the CMS documentary-note system recommendations. (Remember, subsequent references to the same source are abbreviated, just as they are for books and periodicals.)

*Whole website:*

27. David Chalmers, *Zombies on the Web,* http://consc.net/zombies.html, accessed September 7, 2010.

[Note: Site title is italicized. The date the site was accessed is optional in the CMS style, but it is a good idea to include it unless you are sure your instructor does not want it.]

**Online book:**

28. Alasdair MacIntyre, "The Nature of the Virtues," in *After Virtue*, March 2000, http://www.netlibrary.com/EbookDetails.aspx, accessed October 1, 2011.

[Note: If publication information for the print version of the book is known, it should be included in place of the online publication date. For example, Alasdair MacIntyre, "The Nature of the Virtues," in *After Virtue* (Notre Dame: University of Notre Dame Press, 1984), http://www.netlibrary.com/EbookDetails.aspx, accessed October 1, 2011.]

**Journal article (e-journal):**

29. Saul Traiger, "Hume on Finding an Impression of the Self," *Hume Studies* 11, no. 1 (April 1985), http://www.humesociety.org/hs/issues/v11n1/traiger/traiger-v11n1.pdf, accessed February 29, 2012.

[Note: If the website has no page numbers, substitute document divisions such as Preface or Conclusion.]

**Magazine article:**

30. Mike Konczal, "Explainer: Why Do We Need a Volcker Rule?," *Nation*, February 28, 2012, http://www.thenation.com/article/166500/explainer-why-do-we-need-volcker-rule accessed February 29, 2012.

**Other sources:**

The conventions for citing Internet sources that are not simple webpages, periodicals, or books are in flux. Dictionary or encyclopedia listings, blogs, and comments do not fall under the rubrics above. Keep in mind that the point of citations is to enable the reader to locate the source, so provide sufficient information to that end. And as usual, consult your instructor.

Jean Poitras, comment on "Let It Play Out," Adam Radwanski's blog, *Globe and Mail*, comment posted January 14, 2009, http://www.theglobeandmail.com/blogs/wbradwanski, accessed January 19, 2009.

*Stanford Encyclopedia of Philosophy*, "Supervenience," by Brian McLaughlin and Karen Bennett, accessed June 16, 2011, http:// plato.stanford.edu/entries/supervenience.

This site (The Stanford Encyclopedia of Philosophy) sometimes offers stable URLs, which means that the version you are consulting is archived at the stable address, so any subsequent changes will not affect it. If the site you are consulting has this feature, use it.

Daniel Dennett, "The Part of Cognitive Science that Is Philosophy," *Topics in Cognitive Science* 1, no. 2: 231–6, accessed May 13, 2011. doi: 10.1111/j.1756-8765.2009.01015.x

## The MLA Author-Page System

For complete information about this documentation style, consult the *MLA Handbook for Writers of Research Papers*, 7th ed., 2009. Some additional guidelines are available on the FAQ page of the MLA website: www.mla.org/handbook_faq.

In this approach to documentation, the source is typically indicated in the text by the author's last name (either in a phrase or in parentheses) and the relevant page number (in parentheses). The in-text citation refers the reader to a list of works cited, where more detailed information is given about the source. The list is alphabetized according to the authors' last names, with exceptions for sources without authors.

### In-Text Citations

In a typical citation, if the author is mentioned in the text, only the page number is required in parentheses.

> According to MacIntyre, Montesquieu seems to have believed in unshakeable ethical norms while also embracing a kind of ethical relativism (178).

If the author is not mentioned in the text, however, both the author's last name and the relevant page number are enclosed in parentheses.

> Montesquieu seems to have believed in unshakeable ethical norms while also embracing a kind of ethical relativism (MacIntyre 178).

Notice that the parenthetical information appears at the end of the relevant passage. There is no comma between the author's name and the page number, and the parentheses are inserted in front of the period.

Here are some examples illustrating variations on the typical in-text citation.

### Two or three authors:

Moore and Bruder discuss early skepticism and comment on Protagoras (128–9).

Early skepticism and Protagoras are inextricably linked (Moore and Bruder 128–9).

The anthology, however, never did justice to Kant's work, especially the writings of the later period (Bender, Smith, and Atwood 308).

### More than three authors:

Secondary education still seems to deemphasize critical thinking skills (Jones et al. 144–5).

### More than one work by the same author:

The quality of secondary education seems to vary considerably throughout the world (Jones, "Schools" 435).
[Note: Author not mentioned in text. Material in parentheses gives author's last name, abbreviated title, and page number. Quotation marks indicate title of short work such as an article or short story.]

Jones argues that the quality of secondary education varies considerably throughout the world ("Schools" 435).
[Note: Author mentioned in text.]

Phillip Jones argues in *Schools of Tomorrow* that the quality of secondary education varies considerably throughout the world (435).
[Note: Both author and title in text.]

### Entire work:

In *Critical Thinking*, Larry Wright focuses on analytical reading.
[Note: Parentheses and page numbers unnecessary.]

Considerable work has already been done to make analytical reading a main focus of critical thinking (Wright).
[Note: Wright is author of only one work and is not named in sentence.]

### Unknown author:

Some philosophical arguments have never completely retired from the public square ("Philosophical" 92).
[Note: "Philosophical" is an abbreviated title of a short work; work is alphabetized in works cited by abbreviated title.]

### Part of a multivolume set:

The last two hundred years of that period saw very little progress in philosophy and mathematics (Michaels 5: 689).
[Note: Indicates volume 5 and page 689.]

According to Michaels, the last two hundred years of that period were unimpressive (5: 689).
[Note: Author is mentioned in text.]

### Entire volume of a multivolume set:

In the Hellenic period, philosophy seemed to flounder (Henry, vol. 3).

### Authors (of different works) with the same last name:

George Smith offered a powerful argument against federalism (650).

In 1801, a powerful argument was offered against federalism (G. Smith 650).

### Corporate author:

Double-blind controlled trials have shown that large doses of the vitamin are ineffective against cancer (U.S. Natl. Cancer Institute 77).
[Note: In parentheses, name of corporate author is abbreviated if possible.]

According to the U.S. National Cancer Institute, double-blind controlled trials have shown that large doses of the vitamin are ineffective against cancer (77).
[Note: In text, name of corporate author is spelled out in full.]

### Essay or excerpt in an anthology:

In "The Dilemma of Determinism," William James argues that indeterminism makes free action possible (333).
[Note: Page number refers to page in anthology.]

In science and everyday affairs, the notions of determinism and indeterminism are in conflict (James 333).

*Indirect quotation:*

Russell says "no priest or churchman will attend me at my deathbed"
(qtd. in Jones 56).
[Note: Here "qtd. in" (quoted in) is used to signal that the quotation
does not come directly from the speaker quoted but from someone
else quoting the original speaker or writer.]

*Two or more sources:*

The ancient Greeks, however, were a strange mix of rationalism,
mysticism, and paganism (Frederick 22; Hoffman 456).
[Note: Two sources in parentheses separated by a semicolon.]

## Works Cited

The list of works cited is meant to be a complete record of all the
sources used in the writing of a paper. Readers should be able to look
at the list and glean enough information to access every source mentioned. The list has a standardized format, with the sources laid out in
alphabetical order by author's last name or, if the author is unknown,
by the first word of the source's title. Titles of books and periodicals are italicized, and every entry is given a marker indicating the
medium of the source—Web, print, TV, and so on.

The MLA style helps ensure that the authors' names will be readable and easy to find. The first line of an entry is set flush left, but
remaining lines are indented.

Here are some examples of entries for several types of sources.

## Books

*One author:*

Simpson, Carol. *Time's Arrow: The Ancient Conceptions of
Time, Motion, and Symmetry.* Mountain View: Upton, 1980.
Print.

*More than one work by the same author:*

Johnson, Larry. *The Ancient Greeks.* New York: Putnam-Bantam,
2003. Print.
———. *The Hellenic Age.* New York: Oxford-Putnam, 2005. Print.

————. *The Wars of Alexander.* New York: Putnam-Bantam, 1990. Print.

[Note: Three hyphens plus a period in place of name.]

**Two or three authors:**

Smith, Nancy H., and John Morgan. *Great Philosophy in the Ancient World.* Mountain View: Greenland, 1990. Print.

Smith, Nancy H., John Morgan, and J.C. England. *Great Philosophy in Plato's Time.* 4th ed. Mountain View: Greenland, 1966. Print.

**More than three authors:**

Smith, Nancy H., et al. *Philosophy, Mathematics, and Mysticism in Ancient Times.* 5th ed. Mountain View: Greenland, 1967. Print.

**Corporate author:**

National Philosophical Fund. *Employment Prospects for Philosophers.* New York: Huffman, 1970. Print.

**Essay or excerpt in an anthology:**

Sherwin, Susan. "A Relational Approach to Autonomy in Health Care." In *Biomedical Ethics: A Canadian Focus,* ed. Johnna Fisher. Don Mills, ON: Oxford University Press, 2009. 35–43. Print.

**Collection of essays:**

Jones, Nathaniel, and Katharine Wendell, eds. *Philosophy and Religion.* Mountain View: Greenland, 1956. Print.

**Later editions:**

Groarke, Leo A., and Christopher W. Tindale. *Good Reasoning Matters! A Constructive Approach to Critical Thinking.* 4th ed. Don Mills, ON: Oxford University Press, 2008. Print.

**Entry in a reference work:**

"Ethical Naturalism." *Online Dictionary of Philosophy.* U of Edmonton, 2008. Web. 17 Feb. 2009.

[Note: The date of access follows the "Web" medium marker. The URL may be omitted unless your instructor has asked you to provide it, or finding the site would be difficult without it. See discussion on web sources below.]

## Periodicals

*Journal article:*

> Jones, Nathaniel. "Empiricism Revisited." *Philosophy and Religion* 6 (1994): 28–35. Print.

[Note: Citation indicates volume 6, publication date of 1994, and pages 28–35. Article titles are always enclosed in quotation marks; journal names are always in italics or underlined. For journals whose page numbers run consecutively from the beginning of the year to the end through all issues (that is, all pages are in the same volume), the volume number, year, and page numbers are sufficient for identification, as in this example. For journals whose page numbers start at page 1 in each issue, both volume number and issue number must be cited. For example, *Philosophy and Religion* 6.2 (1994): 28–35. The volume number is 6; the issue number is 2. The two numbers are separated by a period.]

*Magazine article:*

> Davis, Samantha. "Ethics in the Workplace." *Harper's* Jan. 1991: 60–3. Print.

[Note: Article title is enclosed in quotation marks; name of magazine is italicized or underlined. Volume and issue number should not be included.]

*Book review:*

> Jensen, Eileen. "When Politics and Philosophy Meet." Rev. of *Commander-in-Chief*, by Jonathan Sosa. *Harper's* Jan. 2001: 56–62. Print.

[Note: Name of reviewer appears first; author of book appears after book title.]

*Newspaper article:*

> O'Kane, Josh. "Who Is Canada Fighting For?" *Globe and Mail*, 15 June 2011, British Columbia ed.: A12. Print.

[Note: Article title is enclosed in quotation marks; name of newspaper is italicized or underlined. Volume and issue number should not be included.]

## Online Works

MLA style requires that it be clear that a source is online, but it does not require that the URL be included, though it recommends it be if the work could not otherwise be easily located. (Of course, you should include it if your instructor requires it.) The current edition of the MLA does not mention DOIs (see the discussion of Online Works above in the CMS section), but your instructor would probably find those an acceptable, or perhaps even preferable, alternative.

**Whole website:**

> Chalmers, David. *Zombies on the Web.* N.p., n.d. Web. 4 May 2011.

[Note: Site title is italicized, followed by the name of publisher (or "N.p." if unknown) and date of publication (or "n.d." if not given). The date of access follows the medium marker ("Web").]

**Online book:**

> MacIntyre, Alasdair. *After Virtue.* Notre Dame UP, 2004. Web. 22 Mar. 2009.

**Journal article (e-journal):**

> Traiger, Saul. "Hume on Finding an Impression of the Self." *Hume Studies* 11.1 (April 1985): n.pag. Web. 28 Feb. 2009.

[Note: After the title, the information is volume and issue numbers (11.1), date of publication or last update, and the page reference (or "n.pag." if there is no pagination). List "Web" as the medium of publication, followed by the date of access.]

**Magazine article:**

> Klein, Naomi. "You Can't Bomb Beliefs." *Nation.* 19 Oct. 2004. The Nation, Web. 22 May 2009.

[Note: Provide the name of the website publisher, or else "N.p." if no publisher given.]

*Other sources:*

The conventions for citing Internet sources that are not simple webpages, periodicals, or books are in flux. Dictionary or encyclopedia entries, blogs, and comments do not fall under the rubrics above. Keep in mind that the point of citations is to enable the reader to locate the source, so provide sufficient information to that end. And as usual, consult your instructor.

> Poitras, Jean. Comment on "Let It Play Out," Adam Radwanski's blog, *Globe and Mail,* comment posted January 14, 2009, http:// www.theglobeandmail.com/blogs/wbradwanski. 19 Jan. 2009.
>
> McLaughlin, Brian, and Karen Bennett. "Supervenience," *Stanford Encyclopedia of Philosophy,* http://plato.stanford.edu/entries/ supervenience. 16 June 2011.

As noted above in the section on CMS style, this site (The Stanford Encyclopedia of Philosophy) sometimes offers stable URLs, which means that the version you are consulting is archived at the stable address, so any subsequent changes will not affect it. If the site you are consulting has this feature, use it.

## The APA Author-Page System

This system has traditionally been used primarily in the social sciences and business, but it is increasingly used in philosophy. Complete details can be found in the *Publication Manual of the American Psychological Association,* 6th ed., 2010.

This documentation style is quite similar to the MLA system; most of the differences are small and rather trivial. For example, MLA convention stipulates no comma between author and page number for in-text citations, but APA requires one, and MLA allows the page numbers to stand alone, but APA requires either "p." (singular) or "pp." (plural) as a prefix. In addition, APA style uses a References list (rather than a Works Cited list), which is organized alphabetically, as in MLA style. A few other minor variations in the References list are that the date of publication comes immediately after the author's name and in parentheses, and book or journal article titles are not capitalized (journal articles are also not enclosed in quotation marks).

Below are examples of a book reference and a journal reference using APA style.

Smith, N.H., & Morgan, J. (1990). *Great philosophy in the ancient world*. Mountain View: Greenland, 1990.

Jones, N. (1994). Empiricism revisited. *Philosophy and Religion* 6, 28–35.

A significant difference between APA and MLA styles is in the treatment of Internet resources in the Works Cited/References section. The APA system requires an accession number be provided, ideally a digital object identifier (DOI) (see discussion under Online Works in the CMS section above). Not all web sources list DOIs, but those that do should be cited by using it, if using APA style. All the usual information is provided, with the last component of a citation being "doi: xx.xxxxxxxxxxxxx." DOIs, like URLs, can be quite long, so copying and pasting is a good idea.

Dennett, Daniel. (2009). "The part of cognitive science that is philosophy," *Topics in Cognitive Science, 1*(2), 231–6. doi: 10.1111/j.1756-8765.2009.01015.x

If there is no DOI for an Internet source, APA convention calls for the full URL to be given.

As mentioned at the beginning of this appendix, a general rule of thumb for citing is to be too scrupulous and informative, rather than to leave the reader unable to find a source.

And (as always!) defer to your instructor!

# ❧ Appendix C ❧
# Grammar Handbook
### by Carolyn Meyer

## Verb Tense Accuracy

Tense refers to the time of a verb's action. Each tense—past, present, and future—has simple, perfect, progressive, and perfect-progressive forms. These convey a range of time relations, from the simple to the complex.

| Tense | For actions . . . | Examples |
|---|---|---|
| Present | happening now, occurring habitually, or true anytime | I walk; she walks |
| Past | completed in the past | I walked; she walked |
| Future | that will occur | I will walk; she will walk |
| Present Progressive | already in progress, happening now, or still happening | I am walking |
| Past Progressive | in progress at specific point in past or that lasted for period in past | I was walking |
| Future Progressive | of duration in future, or occurring over period at specific point in future | I will be walking |
| Present Perfect | begun in past and continuing in present, or occurring sometime in past | I have walked |
| Past Perfect | completed before others in the past | I had walked |

| Tense | For actions . . . | Examples |
|---|---|---|
| Future Perfect | completed before others in future | I will have walked |
| Present Perfect | in progress recently, or of duration | I have been walking |
| Progressive | starting in past and continuing in present | I have been walking |
| Past Perfect Progressive | of duration completed before others in past | I had been walking |
| Future Perfect Progressive | underway for period of time before others in future | I will have been walking |

## Sequencing Past Tenses

When one past action occurred at the same time as another, use the simple past tense in both instances. Use the past perfect tense (*had* + past participle) to show that one past action preceded another.

> When my computer **crashed**, I **lost** part of my essay.
> The power **had come** back on by the time we **returned** from class.

## Shifts in Verb Tense

Shifts in tense are necessary to indicate changes in time frame; however, inconsistent or unnecessary shifts in tense create confusing and illogical sentences.

> ✗ When he **revised** his essay, he **checks** his references. (past/present)
> ✓ When he **revised** his essay, he **checked** his references. (past/past)

## Speculating about the Future, Speculating about the Past

The subjunctive, one of three "moods" in English, expresses action that is improbable or unlikely, as well as requests, wishes, and conditions. It is formed by combining the base form of the verb with the sentence's subject (*work* instead of *works*; *be* instead of *am/are*; *were* instead of *was*). However ungrammatical the subjunctive sounds, use it in formal and mid-level writing in the following situations:

- when clauses beginning with *if, as if, as though,* or *unless* express speculation rather than fact, or describe hypothetical situations that are unlikely;

  If he were to work tonight, he would finish the essay on time. (speculation)

- when clauses ending in *that* express recommendations, wishes, or demands.

  It is important that the university president be [not is] present to greet the dignitaries.

Speculation about action in the past is often difficult to express. In cause-and-effect sentences of this kind, the conditional verbs *could* and *would* belong in the independent clause describing conditions other than they are, not in the dependent *if/unless* clause describing the hypothetical situation that allows for that outcome.

    ✘ If she **would have** telephoned me, I **would have** emailed the information

    ✓ If she **had** telephoned me, I **would have** emailed the information.

## Using Passive-Voice Constructions

The "voice" of a verb refers to whether the subject acts (active voice) or is acted upon (passive voice). The passive voice inverts standard *subject + verb + object* word order so that the original object (the thing that receives the action) becomes the subject of the passive verb.

Active voice • The teaching assistant graded the papers.

Passive voice • The papers were graded by the TA.

Passive voice • The papers were graded.
(The prepositional phrase containing the original active-voice subject is often omitted.)

The passive voice is formed in this way:

a form of the verb *to be* (*am, is, are, was, were, be, being, been*)
+ past participle (for regular verbs, the base form of the verb + *-ed*)
+ (*by* the agent of the action)

In academic writing, the active voice is preferred and should be used whenever possible. There are circumstances, however, in which the passive voice is rhetorically useful.

Use the **active** voice when you need to

✓ write concisely
✓ reveal the doer of an action
✓ deliver positive or neutral news

Use the **passive** voice when you need to

✓ emphasize an action, not who was responsible for it
✓ de-emphasize or soften bad news
✓ take personalities (and their pronouns) out of the picture

## Avoiding Faulty Predication

Subjects and their verbs (predicates) should agree in number and also make sense together.

✗ The **purpose of the study assesses** student preferences.
✓ The **study assesses** student preferences.
✓ The **purpose** of the study **is to assess** student preferences.

The first sentence is incorrect because a *purpose* cannot *assess*. Two other constructions make for similarly awkward sentences:

*is when, is where*
✗ A recession is when the economy experiences a temporary downturn.
✓ A recession is a temporary economic downturn.

*the reason . . . is because*
✗ The reason that we hired her is because she is creative.
✓ The reason we hired her is that she is creative.
✓ We hired her because she is creative.

Use either *the reason* or *because*, but not both, as this amounts to saying the same thing twice.

## Making Comparisons Clear and Logical

Make sure sentences of comparison deliver the meaning you intend. Include all words required to clarify the relationship between the items being compared. Check the correctness of pronouns by mentally filling in implied words and phrases.

   ✘ Students know more about instant messaging than their professors.
(This implies a faulty comparison of *instant messaging* and *professors*.)

   ✔ Students know about instant messaging more than their professors do.
(This sentence compares students' knowledge with professors' knowledge.)

   ✔ Students know more than their professors about instant messaging.

Changing a pronoun can alter the meaning of a comparison sentence:

Scott likes instant messaging as much as me.
(Scott likes instant messaging as much as he likes the writer of the sentence.)

Scott likes instant messaging as much as I.
(Scott likes instant messaging as much as the writer of the sentence does.)

## Using Pronouns with Precision

Pronouns should be of the same case—functioning as subjects or objects—and agree in number and gender with the nouns they replace.

- Pronouns that replace subject words: *I, you, he, she, it, one, we, they, who*
- Pronouns that replace object words: *me, you, him, her, us, them, whom*
- Pronouns that indicate possession: *mine, yours, his, hers, ours, theirs, its*

- Pronouns that indicate reflexive action: *myself, yourself, himself, herself, itself, ourselves, yourselves, themselves*
- Demonstrative pronouns: *this, that, these, those*

### Knowing When to Use *I* versus *Me*

The old taboo against using *me* in combination at the beginning of a sentence—*Tom and me prepared the index*—leads many writers to avoid *me* and use *I* even when the pronoun is supposed to receive the action of the sentence. When two or more people are being referred to, determine what pronoun case to use by temporarily removing the other name with which the pronoun is paired:

> ✗ The new students met with **Alim and I**.
> ✓ The new students met with **Alim and me**.

*Me* is used after prepositions such as *between, after,* and *except*.

> **Except for Lydia and me**, everyone on the floor has first aid training.
> **Just between you and me**, the best time to invest is right now.

## Comma Usage

### Quick Reference Comma Chart

| Use a comma | Don't use a comma |
|---|---|
| • after a dependent clause that begins a sentence: *Although his business failed, he learned a lot.* | • between an initial independent clause and subsequent dependent clause: *He learned a lot although his business failed.* |
| • before a dependent clause added to the end of a sentence as an afterthought: *We should meet next Thursday at 1:00 p.m., if you can spare the time.* | • between modifiers that don't apply equally to the same noun: *A delicious Italian meal was enjoyed by the conference participants.* |

| Use a comma | Don't use a comma |
|---|---|
| • between coordinate modifiers that apply equally to the same noun: *Quinyin submitted a timely, thorough report.* | • before and after relative clauses beginning with *that*: *The report that addressed the failure of the initiative did not assign blame for deficiencies.* |
| • before and after parenthetical expressions, non-essential phrases, appositives, and interjections: *The proposal, which took more than three months to develop, was enthusiastically received.* | • singly between a subject and its verb: *The proposal took more than three months to develop, and was enthusiastically received.* |
| • between items in a series of three or more (the last comma in these lists is optional; it is called a serial comma): *St. John's, Halifax, and Moncton are key markets for our products* | • between two independent clauses joined by *and* that share a subject: *Rinaldo took responsibility for the decline in sales and proposed a new marketing strategy.* |
| • between two independent clauses joined by *and*, each with its own subject: *The impact of reduced health-care benefits on employee morale is considerable, and we will need to discuss the long-term consequences of this policy change at our next meeting.* | |

# Other Forms of Punctuation

## Semicolons and Colons

A semicolon consists of a period sitting atop a comma. Not surprisingly, it performs many of the same functions as the period and comma. Like a period, a semicolon can be used to join independent clauses, especially when they are closely related or when a conjunctive adverb (a word such as *nevertheless, however, moreover, furthermore*) links independent clauses.

New ethics policies were adopted last year; they have been an unqualified success in helping the university promote values of honesty and transparency.

The shipment of computers arrived today; however, it will be several days before the computer system is operational.

Like a comma, a semicolon can be used to separate items in a series. It is especially useful for separating items in cases where one or more of those items contain internal commas.

Our company plans to establish operations in the following centres: Vancouver, the largest market for our sporting goods line; Calgary, the fastest growing market for our products; and Saskatoon, an emergent and underserved market.

A semicolon shouldn't be used to separate dependent and independent clauses or to introduce a list.

A colon is a punctuation mark that is primarily used to set off something to follow. Use it after an independent clause (complete thought) that introduces a list or a long quotation.

Our director of human resources is responsible for overseeing the following areas:
• Recruitment and hiring
• Employee benefits
• Payroll

Do not use a colon following an introductory statement that is a subordinate clause or phrase (incomplete idea).

When proofreading a document
• allow for a "cooling period" before you begin to read
• allow sufficient time to read slowly and carefully
• make several passes over the document

Colons are also used after salutations (*Dear Mr. Evans:*) and between titles and subtitles (*Writing Philosophy: A Guide for Canadian Students*).

## Apostrophes

Apostrophes are used for two principal reasons: (1) to show posses-sion or ownership, and (2) to signal omissions in contractions (*can't, it's, isn't, won't, they'll*). Adding an apostrophe in combination with *-s* to the end of most nouns (not already ending in *-s* and an *s* sound) communicates possession.

Joanne attended the student's seminar.
(a seminar led by one student)

I accepted the committee's decision.
(*committee* is a singular noun)

Marcia is a friend of John's.
(in other words, *Marcia is a friend of his*)

The committee will meet again in two months' time.
(*months* is a plural noun)

Keep in mind, though, that there are many exceptions to this basic rule. When a noun ends in an *-s* or *s* sound, add only an apostrophe unless an extra syllable is needed for the sake of pronunciation.

Joanne attended the students' seminar.
(the seminar involving two or more students)

Two months' extension seems generous.
(*months* is a plural noun)

The business's customer complaints line was deluged with calls.
(extra *-s* added so the word *business* can be pronounced more easily)

Add 's to each noun of two or more nouns when possession is individual.

Paul's and Suleman's papers are excellent.
(Paul and Suleman each wrote an excellent paper; they did not co-write.)

Add -'s to the last noun when possession is joint or collective.

Irene and Madeline's research report has been nominated for a prestigious award.
(Irene and Madeline wrote a research report together.)

## Periods

Periods are used at the end of statements, mild commands, polite requests (that elicit actions rather than verbal answers) and indirect questions (that report asked questions).

**Statement** • The restructuring of our central division led to a year of unprecedented gains.

**Mild command** • Return your completed assignment to me by June 1.

**Polite request** • Please send me a copy of your mission statement.

**Indirect question** • I asked whether they wanted to upgrade their filing systems.

## Question Marks

Question marks are used at the end of direct questions or after a question added to the end of a sentence.

Have you considered taking correspondence courses as a solution to your commuting problems?

The downturn in the real estate market should help our business, shouldn't it?

## Parentheses

Parentheses interrupt the sentence structure, allowing you to add non-essential information or to gently introduce, almost in a whisper, an explanation, definition, reference, or question. Whatever is enclosed within parentheses tends to be de-emphasized, very much the opposite of dashes, which call attention to the set-off text. Some general rules apply: (1) a comma should never be placed before an opening parenthesis, though it may be placed after the closing parenthesis; (2) if a complete sentence in parentheses is part of another sentence, do not add a period to the sentence within parentheses; do add a question mark or exclamation mark if it is required.

The company blamed a high incidence of flaming (the exchange of hostile online messages) for the deterioration of employee morale.

There was a high incidence of flaming (the exchange of hostile online messages), which was blamed for the deterioration of employee morale.

His impressive results on the exam (he had taken a leave of absence to devote himself to his studies) earned him accolades from his instructor.

His unexpected exam results (could he have cheated?) earned him accolades from his instructor.

## Dashes

Dashes are high-impact punctuation—emphasizing the text they set off—but their impact is at its greatest only when they are used sparingly. Use dashes (1) to set off a list from an introductory statement, or (2) to emphasize information that interrupts a sentence. A general rule applies: don't use semicolons, commas, or periods next to dashes.

His latest sales trip took him to the key markets in the Pacific Rim— Tokyo, Seoul, and Taipei.

The practice of shouting—typing messages in all caps—offends many readers.

## Quotation Marks

Quotation marks are used primarily to enclose words copied exactly from a print source or transcribed from overheard speech or conversation. They are also used to enclose the titles of chapters or articles, or to give special treatment to words or letters, especially to unfamiliar technical terms or ironic words. Single quotation marks ('/') enclose quotations that fall within double quotation marks. When inserting a sentence's punctuation adjacent to quotation marks, place commas and periods inside the closing quotation marks, and colons and semicolons outside the closing quotation marks.

"The advantage of online retail," the president said, "is the reduction of storefront expenses."

The term "authentication" has an ever-evolving definition given the development of new systems and technologies.

The article entitled "Teleological Functionalism" is among the best offerings in the most recent issue of *Dialogue*.

---

## Punctuating Sentences: A Quick-Reference Chart

1. Independent clause. Independent clause.
2. Independent clause; closely related independent clause.
3. Independent clause dependent clause.
4. Independent clause, dependent clause that's an afterthought.
5. Dependent clause, independent clause.
6. Independent clause: list of items separated by commas or semicolons.

# Index